Tomasz J. Kopański

BRITISH WW I AIRCRAFT in the Polish Air Force

Mushroom Model Magazine Special

Front Cover
Bristol F2B Fighter of 9 Eskadra Wywiadowcza, Warsaw, August 1920.

(W. Wójcik)

First published in Poland in 1999 by Robert Pęczkowski
Usługi Informatyczne, Orzeszkowej 2/57, 39-400 Tarnobrzeg, Poland
e-mail: robertp@zt.tarnobrzeg.tpsa.pl and
Mushroom Model Publication,36 Ver Road, Redbourn, AL3 7PE, UK.
e-mail: roger.wallsgrove@bbsrc.ac.uk

WYDAWNICTWO DIECEZJALNE SANDOMIERZ
ISBN 83-88006-59-2

Editor in chief . . . . .Roger Wallsgrove
Editors . . . . .Bartłomiej Belcarz
. . . . . .Robert Pęczkowski
. . . . . .Artur Juszczak
Edited by . . . . .Robert Pęczkowski
Page design by . . . . .Artur Juszczak
. . . . . .Robert Pęczkowski
Cover Layout . . . . .Artur Juszczak
DTP . . . . .Robert Pęczkowski
Translation . . . . .Wojtek Matusiak
Proofreading . . . . .Roger Wallsgrove
Aircraft Profiles . . . . .Artur Juszczak
Printed by . . . . .Drukarnia Diecezjalna Sandomierz
ul. Żeromskiego 4, 27-600 Sandomierz,
tel. (+48-15) 832 31 92

Acknowledgements
The author would like to thank the following persons and institutions, for sending photographs and data:
Wiesław Bączkowski
Bartłomiej Belcarz
Jack M. Bruce
Marat Khairulin
Zbigniew Charytoniuk
Jerzy B. Cynk
Andrzej Glass
Jan Hoffmann
Zygmunt Kozak
Stuart Leslie
Wojtek Matusiak
Piotr Mrozowski
Adam Popiel
Wojciech Sankowski
Eyszard Witkowski
Harry Woodman
Waldemar Wójcik
Centralne Archiwum Wojskowe (CAW)
Muzeum Lotnictwa Polskiego w Krakowie (MLP)
Muzeum Wojska Polskiego w Warszawie (MWP)
Polish Instiitute & Sikorski Museum in London (PI&SM)

Table of Contents

GLOSSARY

Centralne Warsztaty Lotnicze (CWL)	Central Aircraft Works
Centralne Składy Lotnicze (CSL)	Central Aircraft Depot
Dywizjon lotniczy	Unit consisting of 2-5 eskadras
Eskadra	Squadron (6-10 aircraft)
Eskadra lotnicza	Air squadron
Eskadra myśliwska	Fighter squadron
Eskadra szkolna	Elementary training squadron
Eskadra treningowa	Advanced training squadron
Eskadra wywiadowcza	Reconaissance squadron
Grupa lotnicza	Air group consisting of 2-5 eskadras (after 13.04.1920 "grupa" was renamed to "Dywizjon")
Lotnicza Szkoła Strzelania i Bombardowania (LSSiB)	Air School of Gunnery and Bombardment
Mechanik (mech.)	Fitter
Obserwator (obs.)	Observer
Oficerska Szkoła Lotnicza (OSL)	Air Officers' School
Oficerska Szkoła Obserwatorów Lotniczych (OSOL)	Oficers' School of Air Observers
Pilot (pil.)	Pilot
Pułk lotniczy (PL)	Air Regiment
Warszaty Centralnych Zakładów Lotniczych (WZCL)	Workshops of the Central Aircraft Works
Ruchomy park lotniczy (RPL)	Mobile aircraft park
Szkoła Podchorążych Lotnictwa (SPL)	Aviation Cadet Officers' School
Wyższa Szkoła Pilotów (WSP)	Advanced Pilots' School

Introduction

November 1918, memorable for the world due to the signing of the Armistice at Compiégne and cessation of hostilities of World War I, was also tremendously important for the Polish nation. All the powers that occupied Poland at the end of the 18th century and divided it among themselves were either defeated (Germany and Austria), or thrown into the chaos of a revolution (Russia). After 123 years of occupation, the Poles could be free again.

From the very first days of its revived existence, the Polish state had a difficult time. To defend its borders it had to fight virtually all its neighbours: Germans, Lithuanians, Russians, Ukrainians and Czechs. Rapid expansion of the army was essential for success.

Air units were among the first Polish military forces established in November 1918. Soon after the air bases of the occupying forces were captured, the Polish-national officers of the former occupant's air forces started to establish air formations. This was a spontaneous

Bristol 20.24 of 10 Eskadra Wywiadowcza at airfield Toruń on 20 September 1920.
(T. Kopański)

action, not co-ordinated by any central authorities, as these simply did not exist at that time.

The first to come into being was the Oddział Lotniczy Lwowa [Lwów[1] Air Unit] formed on 2 November 1918. It was this unit that, on 5 November, flew what would be the first Polish Air Force combat sortie, bombing Ukrainian troops in the part of the city held by them. Two air eskadras arrived at the front line by the end of 1918, while four more were being formed; by July 1919 the air force included fifteen eskadras, and by mid-1920 twenty.

Such rapid expansion of the air force met serious obstacles, though. Lack of aircraft was the principal one, lack of skilled staff being the second most serious. Although by the end of January 1919 the Poles had taken over nearly 800 German and Austro-Hungarian aircraft, the majority of them were only fit to be written-off, and almost 300 had no engines. The remaining ones, after necessary repairs, were gradually transferred to eskadras but their supplies were not sufficient to make up for attrition due to accidents and combat losses, and to provide the required numbers of aircraft per unit.

War-time demolition, as well as lack of an aircraft industry, did not allow mass production of aircraft in Poland. In this situation the only solution was to purchase aircraft abroad.

By the time the spring offensive against the Bolsheviks opened up in the Ukraine in April 1920, Poland had imported nearly 300 aircraft. Most of these, almost 230 machines, were purchased in France (74 Breguet XIVs, 39 Salmson 2A2s, 33 Spad VIIs and 80 training aircraft); the rest came from Austria (38 Albatros D III (Oef)s), Italy (15 Ansaldo Balillas) and Germany

Bristols of 9th Eskadra Wywiadowcza at an airfield near Łuck, September 1920. Some other aircraft of 8 or 14 Eskadras are visible. ***(T. Kopański)***

(over a dozen aircraft of various types, including some 10 Fokker D VIIs).

It has to be added here that most of the French aircraft were part of the seven eskadras that arrived from France in April-July 1919 with the Polish Army under gen. Józef Haller. These aircraft were not transferred formally by the French to the Polish side until September-December 1919. By this time many of the aircraft had been written-off, while some needed a major overhaul. Moreover, many of the aircraft, including a majority of the Spad VII fighters, were so worn that at best they could be used for training, and not without prior overhaul!

Apart from France, Austria, Germany and Italy, Poland also acquired some British aircraft. After the end of World War I and post-war disarmament that country had large numbers of surplus aircraft crated in depots. The authority to sell these aircraft was granted to the well-known aircraft company of Handley Page. In July 1919 a representative of the company presented an offer to the chairman of the Polish Military Purchase Mission in Paris, gen. Jan Romer. After contacting his superiors in Warsaw, in September 1919 gen. Romer sent two representatives of the Polish Air Force to London: por. pil. Marian Gaweł and por. inż. Michał Tłuchowski. These officers evaluated on the ground and in the air the aircraft offered by Handley Page: the Bristol Fighter, DH 9 and SE5a, and sent a report to the Ministry of Military Affairs in Warsaw. Upon receipt of this the Polish aviation authorities asked the British side to display the Bristol Fighter and the SE5a in Warsaw.

Handley Page's team of engineers and pilots arrived by sea in Gdańsk on 1 December 1919. They brought 4 aircraft: two Rolls Royce Falcon III-powered Bristol Fighters and two SE5a's. By mid-December the aircraft had arrived in Warsaw and were assembled there at the end of the month. By 20 December they were joined by a Handley Page HP 0/400 converted to an airliner, intended to be the first of six aircraft of the type to start an airline in Poland.

On 9 January 1920 the fighter aircraft were presented on the ground to the Polish commission led by the Polish Air Force Inspector gen. pil. Gustaw Macewicz. Members of the commission considered the display a good one, and the next day they notified the British that 75 Bristols would be purchased. The SE5a deal was not proceeded with, even though the aircraft gave a good impression.

The reasons behind this decision are not known. Most probably the air force decision-makers did not want the additional complication of introducing yet another aircraft type into service, and with an engine unknown to Polish fitters. At that time the Polish Air Force used no less than 50 aircraft types powered by 20 types of engines.

On 18 January 1920 the Poles decided to increase the Bristol order to 125 aircraft. Unfortunately, unexpected problems arose during further negotiations with the British. These led to several months' delay in conclusion of the contract and resulted in the Poles ordering initially only 75 Bristols, and then 30 more in the second batch, or 20 less than the total originally planned. Details of the negotiations are described more precisely in the chapter related to the Bristol Fighter in Polish Air Force service.

Almost at the same time as the Handley Page pilots displayed their aircraft in Warsaw, another question arose. On 8 January 1920 Gerald Spicer, a representative of the British Foreign Ministry, officially informed the Polish Government that Poland would receive 30 aircraft as a gift: ten DH 9s, ten Sopwith Dolphins, and ten Siddeley Puma-powered Bristol Fighters[2]. The British, disapproving of the "imperial" policy of Poland in the East (war against the Ukraine, and then Bolshevik Russia) decided to transfer the equipment mainly thanks to the support of the coalition leader, Marechal Ferdinand Foch. However, when on 19 January 1920 kpt. pil. Marian Gaweł from the Polish Military Purchase Mission in Paris arrived in London, authorised to collect the aircraft, he met unexpected problems.

One HP-0/400 was given to the Polish Gov. by Handley Page. In this photo the HP is seen at Mokotów airfield in Warsaw 1920.
(T. Kopański)

It turned out that the British Air Ministry had failed to arrange the deal with the Exchequer, and the aircraft could not be collected. Eventually, after some weeks of futile attempts, kpt. Gaweł left London on 14 February 1920 and returned to Paris without the promised equipment.

Things started to change in March 1920, after the misunderstanding was cleared. Later that month the first eight aircraft (two DH 9s and six Dolphins) were shipped on board s/s "Neptun", leaving for Gdańsk on 1 April 1920, the aircraft thence having to go by train to Warsaw.

Three weeks later another batch left for Poland: eight DH 9s and four Dolphins. Meanwhile the Poles were already at an advanced stage of talks with Handley Page, regarding the purchase Hispano Suiza-powered Bristol Fighters. Therefore it was considered that the Puma-Bristols would be of little use. That was why the British were asked to replace these with DH 9s. The British agreed on 19 April 1920, and earmarked a further ten DH 9s for Poland. Loading on board s/s "Neptun" was completed by early May and on 3rd of that month the ship sailed for Gdańsk.

Subsequent deliveries were halted, though. Influenced by the socialist-oriented press which condemned Poland for its war against the "workers'" Bolshevik Russia, anti-Polish sentiments were spreading. On 10 May 1920 a Labour Party rally in Hyde Park voted for a resolution that forbad workers to load military material for Poland. As a result the partly loaded s/s "Jolly George", which was to sail to Gdańsk with artillery guns and ammunition as well as aircraft parts, was unloaded.

In early June 1920 the Poles eventually signed the contract with Handley Page for delivery of 75 Bristol Fighters. For fear of a strike by British workers, the contract included a clause under which the company was responsible for delivery to Gdańsk. Soon after that, on 20 June, the British offered Poland a quick delivery of 50 SE5a's, 50 DH 9s and 50 more Bristol Fighters. The Polish side refused unconditionally to buy DH 9 or SE5a aircraft, but stated that further Bristols might be purchased, provided the original 75 were delivered to Poland in time (between 15 July and 20 August 1920).

Table 1 British Aircraft in the Polish Air Force

Type	Government gift	Purchased from Handley Page	War prize	Other
F4 Buzzard		1		
SE 5a		1		
Sopwith F1 Camel				1
Sopwith 5F1 Dolphin	10			
Avro 504				1
Bristol F2B Fighter		2 + 105		
DH 9	20			
RE 8			1	
1 1/2 Strutter			3	
HP-0/400				1
Combined total	30	109	4	3
Total		146		

Note! The table does not include aircraft displayed in Poland, or used temporarily by Polish pilots, but not taken onto the inventory of the Polish Air Force.

The British fulfilled the contract, which led in August 1920 to an order for 30 Bristols. These machines reached Poland by the end of 1920.

DH 9s, Sopwith Dolphins and Bristol Fighters were not the only aircraft of British production used in Poland. In early 1921 a Martinsyde F 4 Buzzard fighter purchased from Handley Page was delivered to Warsaw. Another fighter, a Sopwith Camel, was acquired from an American pilot of the Kościuszko Squadron. Finally, several more machines of British origin were captured by the Poles during the war against the Bolsheviks between 1919 and 1920.

Bristol F2B Fighter

The first Bristol Fighters to arrive in Poland were brought to Warsaw in December 1919 by the Handley Page team. These were two display machines (including F4409) powered by 275 hp Rolls Royce Falcon III engines.

The British demonstrated their aircraft on the afternoon of 9 January 1920 at Warsaw-Mokotów airfield. They were evaluated by a special commission which included: the Polish Air Force Inspector gen. pil. Gustaw Macewicz, mjr pil. Jan Stachowski, mjr pil. Sergiusz Abżółtowski, por. pil. Jerzy Borejsza, ppor. pil. Antoni Mroczkowski, inż. Klemens Filipowski and inż. Witold Rumbowicz.

One of the flights was made by ppor. Mroczkowski with por. Bolesław Kopyciński as a passenger. The altimeter fitted in the rear cabin indicated that the aircraft reached an altitude of 2100 m in 7 minutes 30 seconds. Trial flights on 9 January proved that the aircraft was fast enough and very manoeuvrable.

On 10 January at 10.00 am the Polish commission assembled again and decided that in view of the successful evaluation 75 Bristol Fighters be purchased. This was not yet a definitive

Ppor. Stanisław Pawluć of 1 Eskadra Wywiadowcza, Białystok, autumn 1920.

(T. Kopański)

1 Eskadra Wywiadowcza Bristol 20.23 during the defence of Warsaw at Mokotów airfield. The aircraft was damaged there on 18.08.1920. Left to right: Unknown stretcher-bearer, por. Skorobohaty, por. Wiltsch, por. Makowski, por. Aleksandrowicz, por. Pawluć, kpt. Domes, por. Gwizdalski, por. Babiński, por. Orłoś, por. Niekraszewicz. (T. Kopański)

decision. On 13 January mjr pil. Stachowski, the Head of the Aerial Navigation Section of the Ministry of Military Affairs, asked mjr pil. Jerzy Kossowski, the CO of V Grupa Lotnicza to fly a Bristol. Kossowski's opinion of the aircraft was as enthusiastic as those of other pilots. He wrote in his report:

"14.I.1920 at 15.00 I performed two flights in an F.2B aircraft; the first one with por. Timme as a passenger, the second with płk. pil. Kieżun. I did all the tricks of higher aerobatics, that is: loops, barrel rolls, wing-overs, wing-slips, sharp turns, etc. The aircraft does all this very eas-

Bristol of 1 or 9 Eskadra Wywiadowcza after "landing" at Mokotów airfield, Warsaw, August 1920. (T. Kopański)

1 Eskadra Wywiadowcza Bristols at Warsaw, Mokotów airfield, 18.08.1920.
(T. Kopański)

ily, without much stressing and it loses very little height (for example during a loop it loses only some 20 m, during a wing-over 20-25 m). The aircraft does not fatigue the pilot, as the controls are very soft (...). the F.2B aircraft gains altitude almost twice as fast as the Breguet, its speed is greater, it lifts bigger loads, and it is stronger. Landing and lifting require stronger airfield and are easier. Being lighter than the Breguet, and having "magneto de port" it takes less time to roll it out of the hangar, and put in motion. Emergency landing due to engine failure is almost impossible, as the F.2B has the world's best engine, the "Rolls Royce".

A similar opinion was expressed by a member of the air commission - mjr pil. Abżółtowski, who added:

Aircraft of 9 and 14 Eskadra Wywiadowcza at the airfield at Chełm Lubelski, September 1920. The Bristol 20.17 of 9 Eskadra Wywiadowcza is clearly visible.
(T. Kopański)

Two photos of the Bristol 20.33 of 10 Eskadra Wywiadowcza after a fatal crash at Brześć airfield on 16.09.1920. Sierż. pil. Karol Biel and ppor. Observer Zygmunt Bem lost their lives, in this accident when returning from a combat sortie.

(T. Kopański)

"I support the opinion of mjr Kossowski. I tried the F.2B aeroplane myself, flying it for 25 min. One of its major advantages is its strong undercarriage and easy landing which, with our poor terrain and little-trained pilots is very important".

After receiving the additional opinions on 18 January 1920 the air commission changed its previous decision, and suggested purchase of 125 Bristol Fighter aircraft.

Further negotiations revealed unexpected problems. It turned out that the British were not willing to sell Poland Bristols with Rolls Royce Falcon III engines, i.e. identical to those presented in Warsaw, but only the variant with 300 hp Hispano Suiza engines. The British standpoint resulted from the fact that production of the Falcon III - standard in RAF Bristols - was not sufficient even for their own needs.

The changed situation required the Bristol to be tested again, this time with the Hispano Suiza engine. To accelerate things it was decided that an aircraft with such an engine would be ferried by air from London to

Pilot por. Wacław Makowski and observer Lt. Robert Vanderauvera (Belgian volunteer), injured by Bolshevik ground fire, in the cockpit of the Bristol no 20.48, (H1279). Białystok 24 September 1920.
(T. Kopański)

Paris and would there be made available to the Polish commission, led by por. Jerzy Borejsza, the air force representative in the Polish Military Purchase Mission.

The Hispano Suiza-powered Bristol despatched by Handley Page did not arrive in Paris until 25 April 1920. The following day it started tests which lasted until 2 May. During these flights the Bristol was flown by Adam Haber-Włyński, a well-known Polish airman. The aircraft proved very good, although it weighed almost 80 kg more than the Falcon III-powered one, and its performance was slightly inferior.

According to por. Borejsza's report, the testing revealed:

"1) Horizontal speed up to an altitude of 3,000 m is 185 km/hour

2) Climbs to an altitude of 3,150 m (10 thousand feet) with a passenger and full tanks, with 50 kg ballast, without guns, in 11 min. 30 sec.

3) Two-hour non-stop flight was satisfactory

4) The vehicle is manoeuvrable, sensitive, good for observation, photography and air combat; less suited for dropping bombs. The vehicle requires a good pilot. Petrol reserve at full throttle (17 thousand revs) - 2 hours; at reduced throttle (15 thousand revs, at which it goes at 185 km[/hour] speed) the petrol is sufficient for 2 hours 40 minutes. (...)

Bristol 20.48 (H 1279) 1 Eskadra Wywiadowcza, Białystok airfield, 24.09.1920. Right to left: por. pil. Stanisław Pawluć, por. pil. Wacław Makowski, kpt. pil. Augustyn Domes (squadron CO - in the car), 2nd Lt. Robert Vanderauvera (Belgian volunteer - in the car). The dog belongs to 2nd lt. Vanderauvera. In the cockpit por. pil. Ignacy Skorobohaty.
(T. Kopański)

The vehicle meets completely the specifications in technical manual received in Warsaw".

After these trials were completed, the final negotiations with Handley Page were held. It was decided that Poland would buy 75 Hispano Suiza-powered Bristols for Ł101,250.- (Ł126,707.- with spares).

The contract was signed on 10 June 1920.

Fulfilment of the contract by Handley Page in August 1920 led to a new contract signed on 14 August, for delivery of another 30 aircraft, additional engine parts, and 60 wheels. In the third contract from 22 September 1920 the company committed itself to delivery of 60 aero engines. Total value of the equipment under the three contracts was Ł185,930.-.

However, the Bristols delivered from Britain after the contract was signed would not be the first in Polish service. They were preceded by the two Bristols left behind at Mokotów airfield by the Handley Page team in January 1920. After the British left the aircraft were probably disassembled and stored at Centralne Składy Lotnicze (CSL). Still the property of Handley Page, they could not be used by the Polish Air Force. However, on 1 May 1920 mjr Aleksander Serednicki, the Head of Field Aviation asked the Minister of Military Affairs that both Bristols be purchased by the Polish Government.

Bristol no 20.26 of 1 Eskadra Wywiadowcza after a nose-over during landing, late September 1920.
(T. Kopański)

This was accomplished in early July. The Bristol F4409, received from the British on 5 July 1920, was given Polish serial 20.1 at Centralne Warsztaty Lotnicze (CWL), while the other (British serial unknown), was to be assembled between 10-25 July, as 20.2. These two aircraft were the only ones in the Polish Air Force to be powered with Rolls Royce Falcon III engines.

Around 20 July the first shipment of Hispano Suiza-powered Bristols purchased from Britain arrived by sea at Gdańsk. The aircraft were shipped to Warsaw and here, in spite of the lack of any documentation, they were erected immediately. This was forced by the extremely difficult military situation of Poland. Bolshevik armies were approaching Warsaw and Lwów, threatening the Polish state. The Polish Air Force suffered from a devastating shortage of equipment, having no more than 50 serviceable aircraft.

The first two Bristols assembled at CWL (20.1 and 20.2) were used in action even before they were allocat-

Crew members of 2 Eskadra Wywiadowcza and their aircraft - Dęblin airfield, autumn 1920
(T. Kopański)

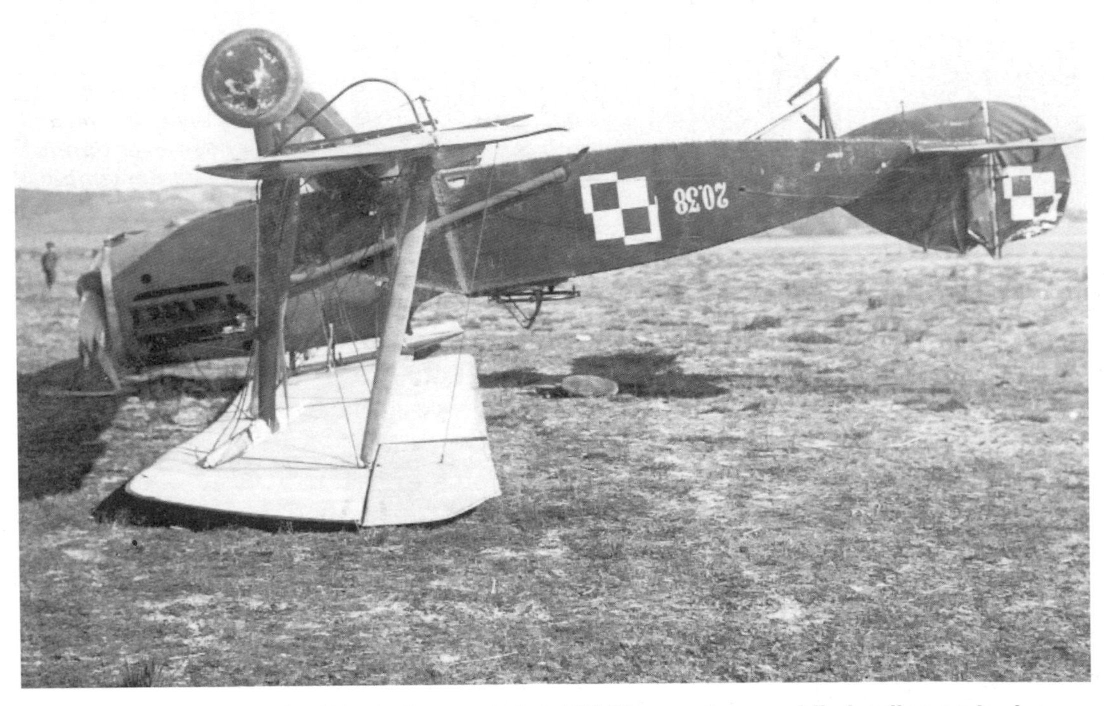

Two photos of 5 Eskadra Wywiadowcza Bristol 20.38 nosed over while landing on Lwów Lewandówka airfield on 13.10.1920 (photo above), and a few minutes after (photo below).
(T. Kopański)

A crew from 10 Eskadra Wywiadowcza, 1920. On the right ppor. Ludwik Samsel.
(Z. Charytoniuk)

Crashed Bristol 20.32 of 9 Eskadra Wywiadowcza, Łuck airfield, 11.12.1920. Pilot ppor. pil. Seweryn Sacewicz was killed.
(A. Popiel)

Crew members of 2 Eskadra Wywiadowcza - Dęblin airfield, October 1920.
(T. Kopański)

ed to any eskadra. On 5 and 6 August ppor. pil. Antoni Mroczkowski with kpt. pil. Julian Słoniewski (as an observer) flew 20.1 on initial combat sorties. They reconnoitred Bolshevik troops in the Wyszków and Ostrów Mazowiecka area and strafed them.

6 August brought the first loss. Ppor. Stefan Żochowski, a 16 Eskadra pilot, with ppor. Stefan Jeznach, a 17 Eskadra observer, were detailed to bomb Bolshevik troops north-west of Warsaw, at Ostrów. Ppor. Żochowski, who had never flown a Bristol before, even to try his hand, did not know the type's peculiar characteristics. He had not been instructed about the use of the adjustable tailplane to balance the aircraft. As a result, aircraft 20.2 overloaded with bombs spun and crashed

A crew from 10 Eskadra Wywiadowcza, 1920. In the observer's cockpit is ppor. Ludwik Samsel.
(T. Kopański)

Workers of the Central Aircraft Works in Warsaw, who assembled Bristol aircraft. Warsaw, Mokotów airfield,1920. In the military hat (4th sitting from left) Eng. Zbigniew Arndt.
(CAW)

upon take-off. The bombs went off and both crew members were killed.

The following day another Bristol was lost, no. 20.1. Due to an engine malfunction the aircraft was forced to land near the front line, north-west of Warsaw, and crashed. The crew, por. pil. Jan Matecki (at the disposal of the Head of Field Aviation) and plut. Franciszek Suchos, an observer of 16 Eskadra, were unhurt and returned to safety on foot.

Meanwhile, Bristols started to arrive in combat eskadras. The first to receive this type of aircraft was 10 Eskadra Wywiadowcza (11 aircraft), followed by 1 Eskadra Wywiadowcza (8) and 9 Eskadra Wywiadowcza (8). After brief conversion to the new aircraft, the units started to enter action: 10 Eskadra on 7 August, 1 and 9 Eskadra Wywiadowcza on 14 August.

During the August fighting around Warsaw each of the Bristol-equipped eskadras flew 30 to 40 combat sor-

Crew members of 3 Pułk Lotniczy. In the centre kpt. obs. Wiktor Szandorowski and ppłk. pil. Sergiusz Abżółtowski. Ławica airfield, Poznań, 1921.
(MWP)

Bristols of 5 Eskadra Wywiadowcza at Przemyśl. Second Bristol from the left (20.44) has its British serial H1275 still visible, 1921.
(T. Kopański)

ties. These consisted mainly of attack missions against Bolshevik troops at Ostrów, Radzymin, Pułtusk, Ciechanów, and subsequently - starting from 17 August - in the area of Mińsk Mazowiecki, Węgrów, Sokołów and Drohiczyn.

In September and October 1920 1 and 10 Eskadra participated in the victorious Battle of Niemen (1 Eskadra was assigned to 2 Army, and 10 to 4 Army), while 9 Eskadra participated in fighting in Wołyń (3 Army), flying dozens of sorties.

Only two Polish Bristols were shot down by the Bolsheviks. 20.12 of 9 Eskadra Lotnicza was the first. It was shot down on 17 August 1920 when attacking a Bolshevik column at Mińsk Mazowiecki. The aircraft crew consisted of pchor. pil. Jan Neumann and ppor. obs. Marian Sioda. Immediately after the forced landing, when shooting at enemy soldiers who approached the aircraft, the observer was wounded. He then ordered his pilot to run, and was himself taken prisoner. Fortunately

The same aircraft, but photo taken from the opposite side of the airfield.
(T. Kopański)

he only spent two days in captivity, and was released by Polish troops entering Otwock.

Bristol F.2B "Fighter" no. 20.3 with a 10 Eskadra crew of kpr. pil. Eryk Szwencer and ppor. obs. Eugeniusz Tromszczyński was shot down on 18 August 1920 during an attack against Bolshevik troops at Sokołów. The aircraft overturned on landing, and the unharmed airmen hid in woods, returning to their Eskadra on 19 August. The retreating Bolsheviks failed to destroy the aircraft, but they removed the observer's machine gun with three magazines, and cut off the harness.

Interesting shot of a Bristol after emergency landing on the road from Ławica to Poznań, 1924.
(W. Sankowski)

Three Bristols crashed during the Polish-Bolshevik war. The first one - on 6 August in Warsaw - cost the lives of ppor. Żochowski and ppor. Jeznach. Two more crashed in September 1920. On 16 September a 10 Eskadra crew of sierż pil. Karol Biel and ppor. obs. Zygmunt Bem was killed at Brześć nad Bugiem in Bristol no. 20.33. Less than ten days later - on 25 September - 9 Eskadra Bristol no. 20.18 crashed when landing at Łuck. Sierż. Jakub Kierojczyk, the pilot, and kpt. pil. Julian Słoniewski, the Eskadra commander who flew as the observer, were both killed.

Bristol 20.24 of 10 Eskadra Wywiadowcza on 10 June 1921 at the airfield at Lwów.
(MLP)

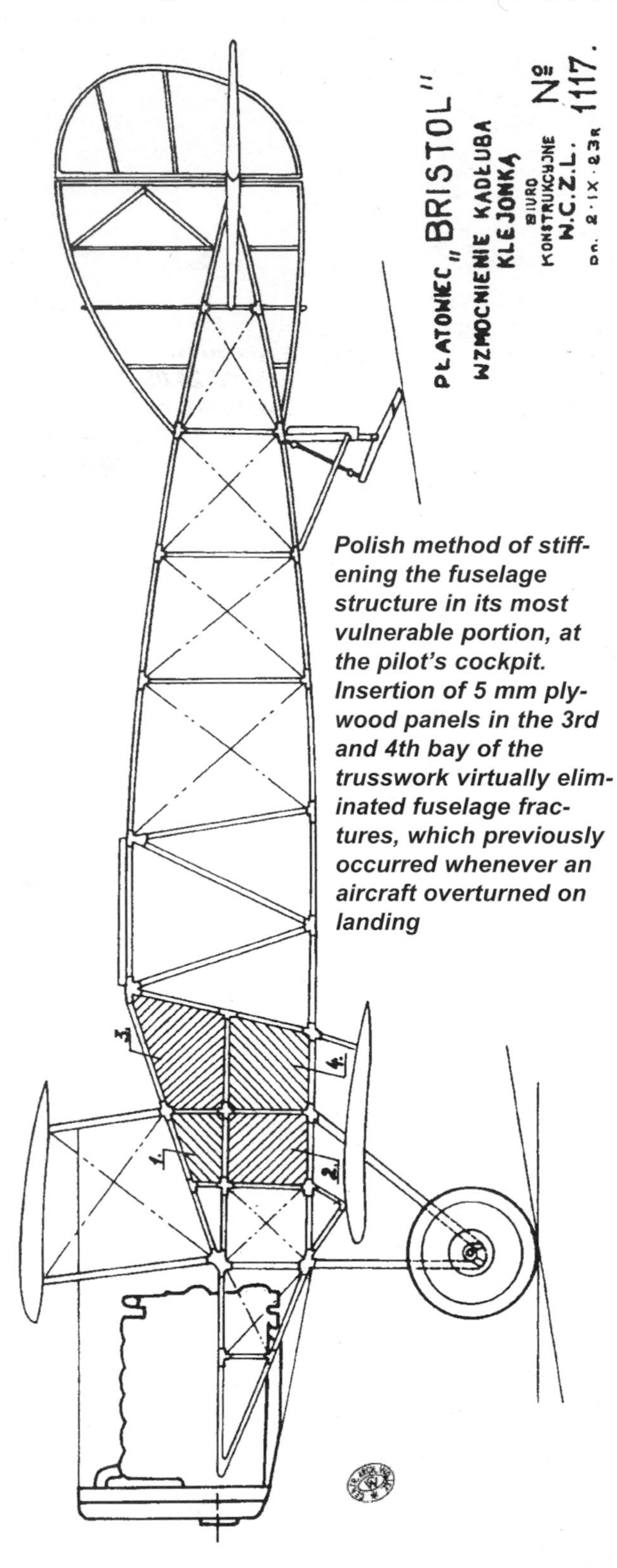

Polish method of stiffening the fuselage structure in its most vulnerable portion, at the pilot's cockpit. Insertion of 5 mm plywood panels in the 3rd and 4th bay of the trusswork virtually eliminated fuselage fractures, which previously occurred whenever an aircraft overturned on landing

During hostilities the Polish Air Force used a total of 40 Bristols in combat, of which 38 were assigned to 1, 9 and 10 Eskadras (see table No 4). When the war with Russia ended, only 11 serviceable aircraft of these 40 Bristols were in units. This was because many aircraft were damaged in forced landings due to engine failures. These failures usually resulted from using incorrect, heavy petrol fractions, additionally polluted with water. The only Bristol to be captured (and subsequently repaired) by the Bolsheviks, no. 20.49 of 9 Eskadra, forced-landed in enemy territory due to poor fuel. This happened on 15 October 1920 at Olesko, and the crew, consisting of CO 9 Eskadra kpt. pil. Bolesław Narkowicz, and ppor. obs. Jan Latawiec, managed to evade the enemy and return to their unit.[3]

Before the Polish-Bolshevik war ended the Aviation HQ decided that two more Eskadras would convert to Bristols: nos. 2 and 5. This decision was influenced by the fact that the shipments of Bristols from Britain were proceeding smoothly, and all 105 aircraft on order arrived in Warsaw by the end of December 1920[4]. 5 Eskadra stationed at Przemyśl received its first two aircraft on 16 September 1920 (20.37 and 20.43), and seven more (20.35, 20.36, 20.38, 20.39, 20.41, 20.42, 20.44) on 27 September. The aircraft were assembled by the Eskadra. The unit failed to

Bristol Fighter

P.u.W 12.5 kg type, bomb loading on Bristol of 10 Eskadra Wywiadowcza. In cockpit, standing ppor S. Łopaciński. Warsaw, August 1920.
(T. Kopański)

Bristol 20.48 (British serial - H1279), 1 Eskadra Wywiadowcza, Białystok airfield 24.09.1920. Left to right pilot por. Gustaw Gwizdalski, observer por. Ignacy Skorobohaty.
(J. B. Cynk)

Aircraft of the Wyższa Szkoła Pilotażu at Grudziądz, ca 1922.
(T. Kopański)

Pilot of 3 Pułk Lotniczy in Poznań kpt. Antoni Woroniecki in Bristol Fighter cockpit. Polish stencil " Flying without passenger or load is not allowed" is visible.

(T. Kopański)

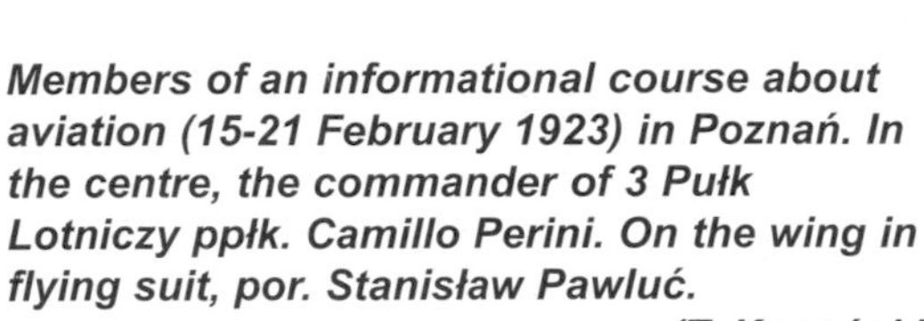

Members of an informational course about aviation (15-21 February 1923) in Poznań. In the centre, the commander of 3 Pułk Lotniczy ppłk. Camillo Perini. On the wing in flying suit, por. Stanisław Pawluć.

(T. Kopański)

Bristol no 20.21 of 1 Eskadra Wywiadowcza, 3 Pułk Lotniczy during exercise in the Wielkopolska region, 1922.

(T. Kopański)

Bristol Fighter

Bristol 20.24 damaged in Warsaw, July 1923. Pilot ppor. Ryszard Bartel.
(T. Kopański)

Pilot and fitters of Eskadra Treningowa, 3 Pułk Lotniczy at Poznań. Ławica airfield, 13 April 1923. Bristol Fighter no 20.48
(T. Kopański)

Bristol crash of 3 Pułk Lotniczy. The crew: por. Flaszyński and por. Bajan escaped unhurt. 2 September 1923.
(T. Kopański)

Table 2 Bristol Accidents in Poland

No.	Date	Aircraft no.	Killed	Location/ Comments
1.	6/8/1920	20.2	ppor. pil. Stefan Żochowski - 16 Esk. por. obs. Stefan Jeznach - 9 Esk.	Warsaw; casualties among passers by
2.	16/9/1920	20.33	sierż. pil. Karol Biel - 10 Esk. ppor. obs. Zygmunt Bem - 10 Esk.	Brześć nad Bugiem
3.	25/9/1920	20.18	sierż. pil. Jakub Kieroyczyk - 9 Esk. kpt pil. Julian Słoniewski - 9 Esk.	Łuck
4.	11/12/1920	20.32	ppor. pil. Seweryn Sacewicz - 9 Esk. (por.obs. Jan Latawiec seriously wounded)	Łuck
5.	3/11/1921	20.47	por. pil. Aleksander Wojciechowski - WSP	Grudziądz
6.	12/1/1923	20.14	kpt pil. Eugeniusz Płuszczewski - 5 Esk. por. obs. Jan Szunejko seriously wounded.	Poznań
7.	16/3/1923	?	por. pil. Roman Marcinkiewicz - 10 Esk.	Poznań
8.	10/8/1923	?	por. pil. Stanisław Korab-Kowalski - 1 Esk. szer. mech. Antoni Wołoczko - 1 Esk.	Poznań
9.	25/9/1923	20.106	por. pil. Adam Świda - 10 Esk. szer. mech. Józef Zachość - 1- Esk.	Poznań
10.	27/10/1924	20.25	kpr pil. Ignacy Żmuda - 4 PL por. obs. Jan Wajda - 4 PL	Poznań
11.	24/9/1927	20.29	por. pil. Ferdynand Pichler - 3 PL.	Poznań; the pilot died 20/12/1927
12.	24/4/1928	20.98	sierż. pil. Stanisław Rybak - OSL sierż. pchor. student - pilot Józef Szneider - OSL	Dęblin

On 22 March 1922, at Wyższa Szkoła Pilotażu at Grudziądz, st. szer. Wacek crashed during landing. His Bristol Fighter 20.69 hit Albatros BII no 2577/17.

(T. Kopański)

Crash at test ground in Biedrusko, near Poznań. Bristol (20.12) of 3 Pułk Lotniczy - 1923 (T. Kopański)

Bristol Fighter no 20.73 of 3 Pułk Lotniczy at the airfield in Bydgoszcz, 1924. (MLP)

Pilot sierż. Leon Ozorkiewicz, (on the right), of 3 Pułk Lotniczy. Poznań, Ławica airfield, 1923. (W. Bączkowski)

Table 3
Bristol serial numbers

Polish serial	British serial
20.1	F4409
20.2	
20.3	
20.4	
20.5	
20.6	
20.7	
20.8	
20.9	
20.10	
20.11	E2713
20.12	H1357
20.13	H913
20.14	H1353
20.15	
20.16	E2734
20.17	E2223
20.18	E2695
20.19	
20.20	H975
20.21	H1355
20.22	H1352
20.23	H1356
20.24	H920
20.25	H983
20.26	
20.27	H1354
20.28	H1273
20.29	H974
20.30	H1358
20.31	H1351
20.32	H1360
20.33	H1350
20.34	H972
20.35	H915
20.36	H1277
20.37	E5217
20.38	H916

Bristol 20.106 of 10 Eskadra Wywiadowcza after fatal crash on 25.09.1923, Poznań - Ławica airfield. Just after take-off, the engine stopped. Pilot tried to turn back, but aircraft spun down from about 40 meters. The crew - pilot por. Adam Świda and fitter szer. Józef Zachość were killed.

(T. Kopański)

Two shots of the Bristol 20.78 during tests with pigeons, winter 1924. Test were carried out at Poznań.
(T. Kopański)

Opposite page middle.
Bristol no 20.10 of 3 Pułk Lotniczy at Poznań ca 1924. Third from the left kpt. pil. Stanisław Pawluć.
(T. Kopański)

Opposite page, bottom.
Damaged Bristol Fighter no 20.25 of 3 Pułk Lotniczy. Possibly the fatal crash of the crew from 4 Pułk Lotniczy- kpr. pil. Ignacy Żmuda and por. obs. Jan Wajda (27.10.1924).
(T. Kopański)

Table 3
Bristol serial numbers

20.39	H1278
20.40	H973
20.41	H1272
20.42	H1270
20.43	H979
20.44	H1274
20.45	H911
20.46	H918
20.47	H919
20.48	H1279
20.49	H971
20.50	H912
20.51	H1310
20.52	H1367
20.53	H1366
20.54	E5229
20.55	H1331
20.56	H1379
20.57	H1301
20.58	H1373
20.59	H1368
20.60	H1308
20.61	H1364
20.62	H1361
20.63	H1307
20.64	H1388
20.65	H1304
20.66	
20.67	
20.68	
20.69	
20.70	
20.71	H1295
20.72	
20.73	E9652
20.74	
20.75	
20.76	H1305
20.77	H1296
20.78	H1275
20.79	

Table 3
Bristol serial numbers

20.80	
20.81	H1288
20.82	H1284
20.83	
20.84	
20.85	H949
20.86	H898
20.87	
20.88	
20.89	
20.90	
20.91	
20.92	
20.93	H954
20.94	
20.95	
20.96	H1287
20.97	H1297
20.98	
20.99	
20.100	H1385
20.101	H956
20.102	
20.103	
20.104	
20.105	H964
20.106	
20.107	

Two shots of crashed Bristol no 20.71 of 3 Pułk Lotniczy at Poznań, 1925. Note the British national marking still visible underneath the Polish national marking, on the right upper wing.

(T. Kopański)

Bristol no 20.29 of Eskadra Treningowa of 3 Pułk Lotniczy, 1926. One year later the aircraft crashed and killed the pilot por. Ferdynand Pichler.

(T. Kopański)

Bristol 20.98 crashed on 24 April 1928 at Oficerska Szkoła Lotnicza at Dęblin. Two airmen were killed, pil. sierż. Stanisław Rybak and a pupil sierż. pchor. Józef Szneider. They were the last two airmen killed in a Bristol crash in Poland.

(R. Witkowski)

Bristol Fighter no 20.22 of Szkoła Pochorążych Lotnictwa at Dęblin before flight, summer 1930.

(T. Kopański)

Bristols at Dęblin, summer 1930.
(T. Kopański)

Bristol no 20.59 at Dęblin 1930. In 1926 this aeroplane was used in Eskadra Treningowa of 3 Pułk Lotniczy, later at Szkoła Strzelania i Bombardowania at Grudziądz.
(T. Kopański)

reach combat capability before the end of the war, partly because some of the aircraft lacked propellers (delayed shipment from Britain).

2 Eskadra, based at Dęblin in October 1920, did not receive Bristols until after the armistice with the Bolsheviks (aircraft nos. 20.52, 20.56, 20.59, 20.60, 20.61, 20.64, 20.68) and obviously failed to participate in hostilities with these aircraft.

The war modified the earlier opinions of the Bristol only slightly. After the end of hostilities the CO 1 Eskadra Lotnicza, kpt. pil. Augustyn Domes, discussed the strong

One of the last Bristols used in Poland, Dęblin 1932.
(T. Kopański)

and weak points of the aircraft types used by his unit (Salmson 2A2 and Bristol Fighter), saying this of the Bristol:

"The Bristol Fighter, while having many of the Salmson's advantages, is absolutely free of many of its shortcomings. This is a perfect example of an aircraft "A tous usages"[5], only incapable of long-range reconnaissance due to lack of bigger tanks, or of bombardment due to insufficient lifting capacity for a destroyer aircraft. It is not quite suited for photography since the strong air

Bristol 20.5 that crashed during test flight after repair, 1.08.1922, Warsaw Mokotów airfield. Pilot kpt. Stefan Pawlikowski, fitter sierż. Ludwik Schultz.
(T. Kopański)

flow and aircraft shudder result in the photographs rarely still. It is best suited for short range reconnaissance and, being very fast and manoeuvrable so that it accepts all sorts of aerobatics and climbs steeply, the Bristol is a perfect aircraft for attacks, and even for dogfights. Its good armament is a warranty of successful results in both cases, while a simple, direct communication between the pilot and observer greatly facilitates any mission.

"The aircraft is very pleasant and, one could say, easy to handle. It does not require much space to take off and land. Only its Hispano-Suiza 300 HP engine failed often. The motor is essentially very good, but is extremely sensitive to even the finest deviations from the state of absolute order which, together with certain not precisely determined caprices (...) often resulted in forced landings."

Soon after the Bolshevik war the Bristols equipped 5 eskadras. However, by 18 January 1921, according to orders of the Supreme Command, the total number of eskadras was reduced by combining the previous ones. Among the Bristol-equipped units 1 and 2 Eskadra formed the new 1 Eskadra, while nos. 9 and 10 became the new 10 Eskadra. These two new units, together with 5 Eskadra, formed VII Dywizjon Wywiadowczy of 3 Pułk Lotniczy at Poznań.

Unknown pilot with Bristol no 20.106 of 3 Pułk Lotniczy at Poznań, 1922.
(A. Glass)

Table no 4. Bristols delivered to eskadras participating in the Polish-Bolshevik war

Unit	Polish serials	Date of delivery	Comments
No assignment	20.1	1/8/1920	crashed 7/8/1920
	20.2	1/8/1920	Crashed 6/8/1920 (ppor. Żochowski †, ppor. Jeznach †)
	20.15	18/9/1920	Crashed 24/9/1920
1 Eskadra	20.21	12/8/1920	Damaged approx. 25/9/1920 (?)
	20.22	13/8/1920	Crashed 26/8/1920 (ppor. Babiński)
	20.23	13/8/1920	Damaged 18/8/1920 (ppor. Wiltsch)
	20.25	15/8/1920	Damaged before 18/10/1920 (?)
	20.26	13/8/1920	Serviceable 18/10/1920
	20.27	14/8/1920	Damaged approx. 1/10/1920 (?)
	20.29	15/8/1920	crashed before 24/9/1920
	20.31	14/8/1920	crashed 24/9/1920
	20.47	16/9/1920	serviceable 18/10/1920
	20.48	16/9/1920	serviceable 18/10/1920
	20.54	25/9/1920	serviceable 18/10/1920
	20.63	23/9/1920	serviceable 18/10/1920
	20.11	9/8/1920	damaged 5/9/1920
9 Eskadra	20.12	14/8/1920	shot down 17/8/1920
	20.13	15/8/1920	damaged 5/9/1920
	20.17	10/8/1920	serviceable 18/10/1920
	20.18	10/8/1920	crashed 25/9/1920 (Sierż. Kierojczyk †, kpt Słoniewski†)
	20.20	13/8/1920	damaged 15/8/1920
	20.30	13/8/1920	serviceable 18/10/1920
	20.32	15/8/1920	serviceable 18/10/1920
	20.49	7/10/1920	landed on enemy side 15/10/1920
	20.3	6/8/1920	shot down 18/8/1920, 26/8/1920 to CWL
10 Eskadra	20.4	3/8/1920	serviceable 18/10/1920
	20.5	8/8/1920	1/9/1920 sent back to CWL
	20.6	3/8/1920	12/8/1920 sent back to CWL
	20.7	7/8/1920	8/8/1920 sent back to CWL
	20.8	4/8/1920	damaged before 17/9/1920
	20.9	4/8/1920	damaged engine 26/9/1920 sent back to IV RPL
	20.10	8/8/1920	damaged engine 26/9/1920 sent back to IV RPL
	20.16	12/8/1920	damaged engine 5/10/1920 sent back to IV RPL
	20.19	12/8/1920	damaged before 10/9/1920
	20.24	12/8/1920	damaged before 10/9/1920
	20.33	14/9/1920	crashed 16/9/1920 (Sierż. Biel †, ppor. Bem †)
	20.34	14/9/1920	Damaged 30/9/1920 (bad engine)
	20.50	2/10/1920	Damaged between 10 and 18/10/1920
	20.58	2/10/1920	Serviceable 18/10/1920
	20.62	2/10/1920	Serviceable 18/10/1920

Bristol Fighter

Fuselage of the Bristol as the hearse during a funeral. The last vehicle for killed airman. 3 Pułk Lotniczy, Poznań 1923.
(T. Kopański)

F2B Bristol Fighter of Eskadra Treningowa, 3 PL Poznań, 1926.

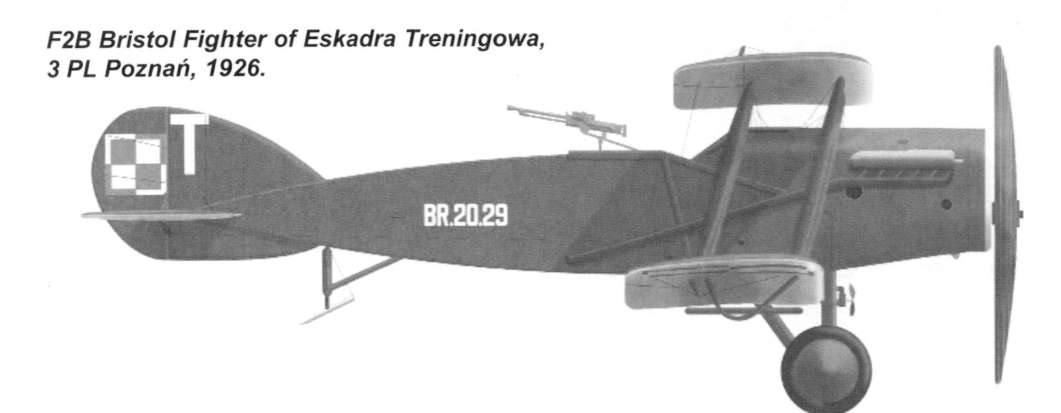

Original document dated 21 March 1921. Allocation of Bristol Fighters after overhaul in CWL

Note that the last Bristol has serial no 20.107.

(CAW)

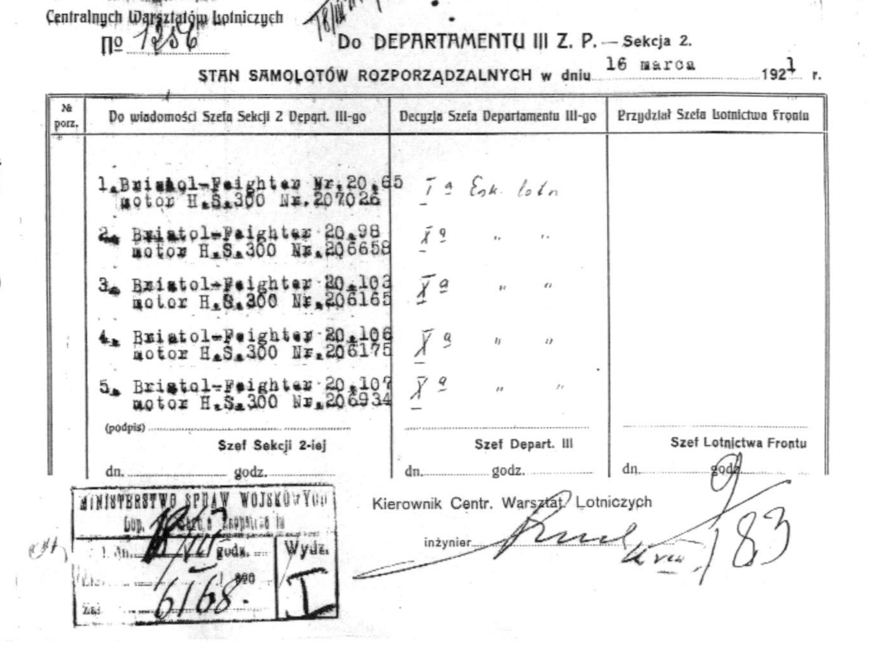

KIEROWNICTWO
Centralnych Warsztatów Lotniczych
Nº 1256

Warszawa, dn. 17 marca 1921 r.

Do DEPARTAMENTU III Z. P. — Sekcja 2.

STAN SAMOLOTÓW ROZPORZĄDZALNYCH w dniu 16 marca 1921 r.

№ porz.	Do wiadomości Szefa Sekcji 2 Depart. III-go	Decyzja Szefa Departamentu III-go	Przydział Szefa Lotnictwa Frontu
	1. Bristol-Feighter Nr. 20.65 motor H.S.300 Nr. 207026	I-a Esk. lotn.	
	2. Bristol-Feighter 20.98 motor H.S.300 Nr. 206658	X-a " "	
	3. Bristol-Feighter 20.103 motor H.S.300 Nr. 206165	X-a " "	
	4. Bristol-Feighter 20.106 motor H.S.300 Nr. 206175	X-a " "	
	5. Bristol-Feighter 20.107 motor H.S.300 Nr. 206934	X-a " "	
	(podpis) .... Szef Sekcji 2-iej dn. .... godz.	.... Szef Depart. III dn. .... godz.	.... Szef Lotnictwa Frontu dn. .... godz. ....

MINISTERSTWO SPRAW WOJSKOWYCH
6168
Wydz. I

Kierownik Centr. Warsztat. Lotniczych
inżynier ....

In 3 Pułk Lotniczy the Bristols were the principal equipment of reconnaissance eskadras for a long time. Their useful lives were prolonged by general overhauls performed from 1921 onwards by the Pułk workshops. Moreover, in September 1923 the design office of Warsztaty Centralnych Zakładów Lotniczych in Warsaw (WCZL), developed a method of stiffening the fuselage structure in its most vulnerable portion, at the pilot's cockpit. Insertion of 5 mm plywood panels in the 3rd and 4th bay of the trusswork virtually eliminated fuselage fractures, which previously occurred whenever an aircraft overturned on landing. Thanks to this Bristols were used in 3 Pułk Lotniczy in the first line until they were replaced by Potez XV aircraft in mid-1925. In early February of the following year the Pułk still had 55 Bristols stored, including 4 earmarked to be written-off. After the necessary inspections in the spring of 1926 several machines were made serviceable again, and went to the Eskadra Treningowa of the Pułk, while the remaining ones were transferred to flying schools.

The Bristols had been used in these schools from late 1920. Oficerska Szkoła Obserwatorów Lotniczych (OSOL) at Toruń used them for observer training, while Wyższa Szkoła Pilotów (WSP) at Grudziądz - used them for flying training. In November 1925 the WSP was reformed into the Oficerska Szkoła Lotnicza (OSL) and after it moved to Dęblin in April 1927, the Lotnicza Szkoła Strzelania i Bombardowania (LSSiB) was established at Grudziądz. Thus by the end of 1925 a number of Bristols reached Dęblin; while the rest were kept by the LSSiB, where they were used for bombing and air gunnery training, and for H-target towing until early 1930s. These aircraft, similar to those used at Dęblin, were most usually equipped with twin Vickers F observer's machine guns.

Around 1930 the Bristols were withdrawn from the Grudziądz school and assembled at the Szkoła Podchorążych Lotnictwa (SPL), established in 1928 at Dęblin from the previous OSL. The Dęblin school was the last user of these aircraft. In mid-1929 it still had 29 of them, but only some of these were serviceable[6]. Two years later, on 1 April 1931 Poland had a total of 47 Bristol Fighters, including 10 serviceable ones (8 of these at Dęblin). Among the remaining 37 machines,

20 disassembled Fighters were in storage, and 17 more awaited being written-off due to damage or wear. In the autumn 1932 the last Bristols used until that time at Dęblin for air gunnery training were withdrawn from use.

Bristol of 3 Pułk Lotniczy, Poznań, 1923-1924.

Sopwith Dolphin

Sopwith Dolphins arrived in Poland in two batches, in April and May 1920. The first shipment, consisting of six aircraft, after a month's storage in Warsaw, was despatched in mid-May to Lwów - for III Dywizjon Lotniczy. On 19 May the machines were received by the Lwów-based III Ruchomy Park Lotniczy (III RPL), and their assembly started. The Dolphins were in good shape, with the exception of aircraft no. J162 in which the RPL personnel had to fix nearly 60 perforations, and repair other minor damage.

The British aircraft failed to raise enthusiasm among the Poles. On 25 May 1920 the Head of the Field Aviation mjr pil. Aleksander Serednicki reported in his

Table no 5. Sopwith Dolphin - Shipments to Poland

Ship Departure from London	Shipment	Arrival at Gdańsk	Arrival at Warsaw	Arrival at Lwów
s/s "Neptun" 1/4/1920	6 Sopwith Dolphins: J153, J162, J169 J178, J181,J7128	approx. 10-15/4/1920	approx. 19/4/1920	19/5/1920
s/s "Warszawa" 21/4/1920	4 Sopwith Dolphins: J39, 151, F7120 E4815 - probably	4/5/1920	approx. 10/5/1920	-

Dolphin of No. 87 Squadron RFC at Petite Synthe, France in March 1918.
(J.M. Bruce/S. Leslie.)

No photos of Polish Dolphins have been found yet.

signal to 2nd Section of III Department of Aerial Navigation:

"General reports of pilots receiving the S. Dolphin aircraft quote that these aircraft were withdrawn from use by the Allies as being dangerous for the pilot. It is asked kindly to investigate:

1) who received these aircraft,
2) to ban flying on these aircraft and to use them in some other way".

On 27 May 1920 a shipment of ten DH 9s arrived at Lwów. It was then that the decision was made to halt assembly of the Dolphins - this was acknowledged to the Head of Field Aviation in a signal of 4 June by kpt pil. Stefan Bastyr, the 6 Army's Head of Aviation.

In early July the Dolphins were sent back from Lwów to Warsaw. In view of the dramatic situation at the front line, and the general lack of equipment, previous orders were amended. It was decided to transfer these aircraft to 19 Eskadra Myśliwska tasked with air defence of Warsaw from Bolshevik attacks.

Four Dolphins held in Warsaw upon their arrival from Gdansk were assembled here in late July. They received Polish serials 21.01, 21.04, 21.08, and 21.09. Six machines sent back from Lwów were to be assembled at the CWL between 30 July and 10 August. They received serial numbers 21.02, 21.03, 21.05, 21.06, 21.07, and 21.010. Upon assembly the aircraft were test flown by Bolesław Skraba, the CWL contract pilot.

19 Eskadra which only had 5 pilots at that time, received the first Dolphins in early August. Initially they were used for patrolling the Warsaw area, and subsequently - when the Bolshevik threat to the capital of Poland was found to be nil - for reconnaissance and ground attack sorties.

First reconnaissance sorties were flown on 4 and 5 August by pchor. pil. Eugeniusz Guttmejer in 21.08. He attacked the Bolshevik rear and cavalry in the area of Ostrów Mazowiecka-Zambrów.

The Sopwith of ppor. Zbigniew Bieniawski (believed to be 21.01) was shot down by ground fire during a combat sortie on 8 August. The pilot managed to land on the Polish side of the front line, damaging his machine.

Two combat sorties were flown on 13 August by pchor. Guttmejer. During one of those the pilot strafed a Bolshevik car on the bridge across Liwiec river at Owsianka. The car, with the crew wounded or killed, fell into the river.

On 14 August 19 Eskadra lost another aircraft. During an attack by two machines against Bolshevik troops at Ostrów, the aircraft of pchor. Guttmejer (21.08) received a hit in the engine. The pilot managed to nurse it to his own lines and crash-landed at Żabki. His Sopwith overturned and was damaged.

On 15 August four pilots of 19 Eskadra: por. Antoni Mroczkowski (Sop. 21.09), plut. Edward Waleriańczyk (Sop. 21.02), ppor. Bieniawski (Sop. 21.04) and pchor.

Dolphin No. 124 of 2 Fighter School at Maraske in Yorkshire. (J. M. Bruce / S. Leslie)

Dolphin of No. 10 Training Squadron at Harling Road, Norfolk. (J. M. Bruce/S. Leslie)

Guttmejer (Spad VII) attacked Bolshevik positions at Radzymin. During the combat aircraft no. 21.09 had its propeller shot through eight times due to faulty synchronising gear. Guns jammed in the other three machines.

On 17 August aircraft of the eskadra participated in an attack against enemy troops at Mińsk Mazowiecki. Plut. Waleriańczyk's aircraft had its propeller shot through several times, so that upon landing one blade fell off completely.

On 18 August por. pil. Stanisław Gołębiowski and pchor. Guttmejer strafed a Bolshevik airfield at Ostrów. Soon after that the Russians left the location, probably upon learning of the withdrawal.

On 20 August plut. Waleriańczyk encountered and strafed enemy infantry and rear elements withdrawing north-west of Warsaw (Komorów-Białystok road). His Sopwith's elevators were hit by several bullets.

During the Battle of Warsaw 19 Eskadra Myśliwska pilots flew some 15 Sopwith sorties.

At the end of August 1920, after the Bolsheviks withdrew from Warsaw, 19 Eskadra had only one serviceable Sopwith left, no. 21.04. By 14 September 1920 the aircraft had flown 16 hours. During August 1920 the Sopwith no. 21.09 had 18 hours 10 minutes flying time, and Sopwith no. 21.010 - 10 hours 10 minutes.

In early September 1920 all the Dolphins used previously by 19 Eskadra were stored at CWL. They could not be made serviceable due to faulty synchronising gear and lack of propellers.

In mid-September 19 Eskadra started to receive new Spad XIII fighters. The Sopwiths were then offered to the American pilots of 7 Eskadra Myśliwska "Tadeusz Kościuszko". Maj. Cedric Faunt le Roy, the unit CO, signalled on 19 September to the Head of Field Aviation that his pilots would rather continue flying the Albatros (Oef) DIII and Ansaldo Balilla aircraft, and were not interested in the Dolphins.

Eventually in early October 1920 the three serviceable Dolphins were allocated to 18 Eskadra in the process of conversion to single-seat aircraft at Grudziądz (previously it had been a reconnaissance unit). Aircraft nos. 21.04, 21.09, 21.010 were delivered there. In March 1921 the eskadra moved to Dęblin, where it would amalgamate with 19 Eskadra. By that time it only had one Sopwith, and five Spad XIIIs. Soon the Sopwith was sent back to CWL.

Apart from the Poles, Ukrainian pilots also flew Sopwith Dolphins. In October 1920 they formed 1 Zaporoska Eskadra Lotnicza in Warsaw under kpt. pil. Żachowski. The unit was equipped with two Sopwiths: 21.01 and 21.03, as well as four Albatros J.I and one LVG C.V. It is believed that these aircraft were marked with Ukrainian emblems in form of squares divided diagonally into two equal triangles, blue and yellow. The Ukrainian unit went to the Bolshevik front after the Poles signed an armistice with the Bolsheviks on 24 October. The Ukrainian army was soon defeated by the Russians, and within a month it withdrew to Poland. On 23 November 1920 the Eskadra aircraft flew from their base at Wołoczyska to Lwów. It is not known whether the Ukrainian pilots ever flew combat sorties on Sopwiths, but even if they did not many could have been flown. On 22 February 1921 the Ukrainians formally gave up their aircraft to the Polish side at Bydgoszcz. It was probably then that both Dolphins were sent back to Warsaw.

In April 1921 CWL stored a total of 5 Sopwiths. The first of these, no. 21.08, was overhauled by mid-May and ready for test flying. Unfortunately, the CWL test pilot Bolesław Skraba refused to test fly it, on the grounds that due to its unorthodox layout the aircraft was dangerous, and if overturned on landing it would expose the pilot to great risk of injury. According to Skraba:

"The pilots in general decided not to fly the above aeroplanes, or to damage them on the first available occasion".

It is possible that this threat was fulfilled, as by early 1922 CWL only had four Dolphins awaiting a general overhaul. Due to the lack of pilots willing to fly them, the overhauls were never undertaken. At that time the Warsaw and Lwów Technical Universities tried to obtain two Dolphins as educational airframes for aircraft engineering studies. In August 1922 an air force representative requested that the universities overhaul both aircraft at their own cost to airworthy status. This condition could not be met and the universities gave up their attempts. At the turn of 1922 all remaining Sopwith Dolphins were earmarked to be written off.

Conjectural apperance of Sopwith Dolphin 21.08 of 19 Eskadra Myśliwska.

Martinsyde F4 Buzzard

In reply to Polish Air Force interest in the F4 Buzzard, Handley Page shipped one aircraft of the type to Poland in January 1921. Initially it was serialled H7780, but before leaving Britain it received the civil registration G-EAWE (14 January 1921).

The ferry flight to Poland in several stages took from 21 - 29 January 1921. Soon after arrival in Warsaw, most probably in early February 1921, the aircraft was displayed to a Polish air commission under ppłk. pil. Antoni Buckiewicz. Three demonstration flights were made. F/Lt Percy from Britain flew the first two, and ppor. Stefan Pawlikowski the third one.

The Polish commission compared the Buzzard to the Balilla and Spad XIII used in Poland at that time. It was found that the British aircraft was more stable in flight and could turn at a radius equal to or even smaller than the fighters used in Poland. Also the take-off and landing speed of 80-100 km/h was estimated higher than that of the Balilla. On the other hand, barrel rolls were slower, and with some resistance.

In spite of the generally favourable test results of the aircraft, the Poles did not decide to purchase any more of these fighters for their eskadras. The reason behind this decision is not known.

Later the display machine was bought from Handley Page. The exact date of the deal is not known, but it could be as late as 1923.

It is known that the aircraft was test flown in Warsaw on 23 May 1923. On 19 June of that year it was transferred from the Eskadra of Experimental Section of the Military Air Research Centre. In early August the aircraft took part in the 2nd Air Tour of Poland. It was flown by kpt. pil. Józef Hendricks. Due to an engine failure it with-

F-4 Buzzard when assigned to the CO of PAF gen. Włodzimierz Zagórski.
(A. Glass)

drew from the competition during the first stage of the Tour, on 4 August 1923.

In early 1925 the aircraft was taken over by gen. pil. Włodzimierz Zagórski, the AOC Polish Air Force (Head of the IV Department of Aerial Navigation). He used it until May 1926. During that period the aircraft had a striking finish of horizontal red-and-white striping

After the coup d'etat of Marshal Józef Piłsudski in mid-May 1926, gen. Zagórski ceased to be the AOC PAF. His aircraft remained in service only a little longer. On 9 July 1926 it was flown by por. pil Bohdan Butkiewicz, an instructor of the Eskadra Szkolna in 1 Pułk Lotniczy. During landing at the Mokotów airfield he crashed the aircraft, suffering injuries. The accident was caused by a broken undercarriage cable which resulted in the fighter overturning, and sustaining serious damage. In all probability the aircraft was never repaired.

F-4 Buzzard at Mokotów airfield in Warsaw, summer 1925.
(T. Kopański)

Sopwith Camel

In September 1920 a single Sopwith 1F.1 Camel arrived in Poland. This was aircraft no. F5234, manufactured by March, Jones & Cribb in Leeds, powered by Bentley Vickers BR-1 engine no. 3023.

The aircraft was the private property of Lt. Kenneth Murray, one of the American pilots of 7 Eskadra Myśliwska "Tadeusz Kościuszko". It arrived at Lwów, where the eskadra was based, on 14 October 1920, too late to participate in the war against the Bolsheviks. It was assembled within a few days, and around 20 October it flew its first 20 minute test flight. By the end of November it had flown 18 hours and 7 minutes in the hands of various pilots. In December the aircraft was not used, most probably due to the hard winter.

During the early months of 1921 it was flown much less frequently, so that by the end of May it had only flown 1 hour and 20 minutes. In mid-May, before the American volunteers went back to the USA, the aircraft was bought by the Polish Government.

Sopwith F.1 Camel no F5234 with 7 Eskadra Myśliwska (Kościuszko) emblem on Lewandówka airfield, Lwów. Standing by the plane is its private owner, Lt Kenneth Malcolm Murray. He was an American volunteer.
(J.B. Cynk)

Camel together with Balilla and Albatros (Oef) DIII at Lewnadówka airfield, Lwów. Aircraft with Polish national markings. Lt Murray sold that plane to the Polish Gov. in the spring 1921.
(MLP via Belcarz & Pęczkowski)

The aircraft was damaged by Ludomił Rayski, later Commander of PAF during his first flight on that type.
(T. Kopański)

Its career in the Polish Air Force was short, though. In the summer of 1921 mjr pil. Ludomił Rayski, the Szef Technical Head of the III Department of Aerial Navigation, while visiting the Lwów airfield, decided to make a test flight in the Camel. On 1 August 1921, soon after the take-off, when the fighter was at an altitude of some 100 m, its engine suddenly stopped. During a forced landing the Camel crashed, and its pilot was seriously hurt. The aircraft was not repaired.

At present the Muzeum Lotnictwa Polskiego (Polish Aviation Museum) at Cracow has the fuselage of Sopwith F.1 Camel no. B7280. The aircraft, of no. 210 Squadron RAF, was shot down by the Germans on 5 September 1918. Later on it was exhibited in the Berlin Aviation Museum. During WW2 it was evacuated with a number of other exhibits to Polish territory. Taken over by the Poles it went to Cracow, where it was restored during 1990-1991.

SE 5a

Two SE 5a aircraft were brought to Poland in December 1919 by the Handley Page team (together with the two Bristol Fighters). On 9 January 1920 one of the SE 5a's was demonstrated in Warsaw to the Polish air commission and made a good impression. This impression was improved after a competition between the SE 5a, a Fokker D.VII and an Ansaldo Balilla. The SE 5a, flown by the factory pilot of CWL, ppor. Antoni Mroczkowski, won. Unfortunately, on 2 February 1920 the aircraft crashed on landing after another display flight. Ppor. Mroczkowski wrecked the aircraft, and broke both hands.

At the moment of the accident the aircraft was still the property of Handley Page and therefore was not included in the listings of Polish Air Force aircraft. The accident affected the decision of the Polish commission which, as

Te Se-5a was one of the two aircraft shown to Polish aviation authorities in 1920. This photo was taken in January 1920 at Mokotów airfield. ***(T. Kopański)***

The same aircraft during the trials.
(T. Kopański)

mentioned previously, opted for purchase of the Bristol Fighter, but not of the SE 5a.

After the British team left Warsaw, its aircraft (an SE 5a and two Bristol Fighters) were left in Poland. As property of Handley Page they could not be used by the Polish Air Force. They were therefore dismantled, and subsequently stored at the CSL.

In June 1920, in view of the shortage of equipment in the Polish Air Force, mjr pil. Aleksander Serednicki, the Head of Field Aviation at the Supreme Command, asked the Minister of Military Affairs that the fighter left in storage be purchased from Handley Page. This was aircraft no. F9135, built by Vickers Ltd at Crayford (Hispano Suiza engine no. 3684). The aircraft was soon pur-

In the beginning of February 1920 the SE-5a made by Martinsyde was shown to army authorities. During landing on a snow covered airfield the aircraft was completely destroyed by ppor. Antoni Mroczkowski. 2 February 1920.
(W. Bączkowski)

chased and on 5 July 1920 its assembly was started at the CWL. Upon completion it received Polish markings and the CWL serial number 12.01.

On 8 July 1920 Maj. Cedric Faunt le Roy, the OC of 7 Eskadra Myśliwska "Tadeusz Kościuszko" formed of American volunteers, who somehow learned about the SE 5a being erected, asked the Head of Field Aviation to allocated the fighter to his unit. The assignment was approved on 13 July. The following day the SE 5a, flown by kpt. pil. Stefan Ciecierski, left for Kowel. On 15 July Ciecierski landed at Hołoby landing ground, where 7 Eskadra was based. Then, after a few hours respite, he took of in the SE 5a for a reconnaissance sortie in the Łuck area. At Kolonia Podhajce village he saw Bolshevik cavalry and attacked it. Unfortunately, a well aimed shot from the ground damaged the engine of the aircraft and Ciecierski was forced to land in enemy territory, the aircraft overturning on the ground. The pilot was taken prisoner, and the crashed aircraft was set on fire by the Bolsheviks.[7] The burnt-out wreck was found by Polish troops in September 1920 after they liberated Łuck.

After the news of SE 5a being missing was received at CWL, the engine and other parts from the fighter that had crashed in February 1920, regarded as spares for 12.01, were transferred for storage at CSL on 23 July.

Second SE-5a, after receiving Polish no 12.01, was sent to 7 Eskadra Myśliwska, at the front. The photo was taken on 15 July 1920 at Hołoby airfield. Close to the prop is kpt. Stanisław Ciecierski, the pilot who was shot down in that plane during its first combat mission. The pilot become PoW, but later escaped.

(J.B. Cynk)

In 1926 two SE 5as were used in Poland. Both were used for skywriting. Both belonged to an ex RAF F/Lt G. C. Worledge (Savage Skywriting Co.). In this photo is G-EBIC in the summer of 1926, at the airfield at Lwów.
(T. Kopański)

In May 1926 two more SE 5a's arrived in Poland. They were not the property of the Polish Air Force, however, but of Savage Skywriting Co., owned by Mr James G. C. Worledge. The aircraft, fitted for smoke sky-writing, were registered as G-EBIC and G-EBXC. They were used for advertising various products for at least one season. They flew in Warsaw, Cracow, and Lwów, among others.

The other SE 5a also belonged to Savage Skywirting Co. with British registration G-EBXC.
(MLP via Belcarz and Pęczkowski)

Airco DH 9

In early 1920 20 DH 9 aircraft arrived in Poland. They were shipped from Britain to Gdańsk by sea and then went to Warsaw (and Lwów) by train. Details are given in table no 6.

The first two DH 9s arrived from Gdańsk at Warsaw at the end of April (together with six Sopwith Dolphin fighters). Less than a month later, without having been uncrating, they were despatched to Lwów for III Dywizjon Lotniczy. Soldiers of III RPL collected these machines on 19 May 1920. After evaluating the contents, a commission of the RPL officers decided that in all probability not a single aircraft could be made serviceable, due to their poor technical condition.

Nevertheless, workers led by the RPL commander, por. Władysław Toruń, started assembly. Aircraft no. F1173 had almost 50 holes that needed repair. The aircraft crashed during its first flight around 8 June. In view of this, assembly of the second aircraft (H4279) was abandoned, as this was in equally bad shape. In all probability the aircraft was earmarked to be written-off.

In mid-May 1920 another shipment of aircraft reached Warsaw: eight DH 9s and four Sopwith Dolphins. The aircraft were in very bad condition, so instead of being assigned to units, they were sent directly for storage at CSL. They would not enter service until after the Polish-Bolshevik war, and after a thorough overhaul.

Another batch of ten DH 9s and five spare Siddeley Puma engines was despatched from Gdańsk directly to Lwów. On 27 May 1920, upon their delivery, it was decided at III RPL that assembly should start immediately. The Poles were assisted by a British engineer who, however, had never worked on a DH 9 before!

Assembled at Lwów the DH-9 no H4315 belonged to 5 Eskadra Wywiadowcza, seen here before flight at Tarnopol. The photo was taken in July 1920 at Lewandówka airfield, Lwów.
(T. Kopański)

According to the plans of CO III RPL, all machines would have to be ready for collection on 15 June 1920, in order to be delivered as soon as possible to eskadras at the Bolshevik front. It turned out, though, that some of the aircraft (three or four) would not be made serviceable due to serious technical problems. These machines were therefore stored at III RPL, and then despatched to CSL in Warsaw.

On June 1920 DH 9 no. D1278 crashed during the first flight performed by plut. Mieczysław Błotny, a III RPL pilot. The airman survived, although he was badly hurt.

The remaining machines were test flown by pilots of 5 and 6 Eskadra Wywiadowcza from III Dywizjon Lotniczy of 6 Army, specially recalled from the front line to Lwów. After a few conversion flights on 4 July they left for the front-line airfield at Tarnopol. Most probably each

The same aircraft as shown in the photos on the opposite page was later used in September 1920 by 6 Eskadra Wywiadowcza. Note especially the early Polish national markings without outline. The British serial no. is also visible.
(T. Kopański)

Two shots of unfortunate landing of the DH-9 no H4315 after a recce flight in July 1920.
(T. Kopański)

eskadra received three aircraft. In the case of 5 Eskadra these included DH 9 nos. H4315, H5721 and probably D1273. 6 Eskadra was assigned nos. D1325, D5733 and probably D1275.

The fates of two of 6 Eskadra's DH 9s are known. One of these, D5733, crashed on 18 July after having flown only a few combat sorties. The accident took place when returning from a reconnaissance mission, when the pilot was forced to land near Krasne (Gliniany village) due to engine failure.

The other aircraft, D1325, was sent back to III RPL on 25 July for engine repair and fitment of a new fuel pump (Benz type). Fate of the third aircraft is unknown,

DH-9 of 6 Eskadra Wywiadowcza in a hangar at Lwów airfield. In the cockpit is a fitters of 7 Eskadra Myśliwska szer. Adam Babiński. (T. Kopański)

perhaps it was damaged during a ferry flight to Tarnopol on 4 July.

The 5 Eskadra DH 9s also failed to serve for longer. These were flown, among others, by por. pil. Władysław Kalkus and ppor. pil. Ludwik Nazimek. All the machines left the unit before the end of July. DH 9 no. H4315 overturned during a crash-landing, and was sent back to III RPL, and thence to Warsaw. D1237 alighted on the Seret river due to engine failure, while H5721, damaged in unknown circumstances, was also sent back to RPL at Lwów.

DH-9 , H5721 of 4 Eskadra Wywiadowcza at auxiliary airfield close to Tarnopol, early July 1920. (W. Bączkowski)

The same aircraft as on the opposite page, bottom, but this time at Lwów airfield.

(T. Kopański)

In the III Dywizjon the DH 9s were considered to be good, strong airframes with poor engines (Siddeley Puma). Apparently the fuel pump was their weak point.

On 1 September 1920 5 Eskadra received D1275, repaired at III RPL. Since the unit was soon going to receive Bristol Fighters, six days later the DH 9 was transferred to 6 Eskadra. It remained with the latter unit rather briefly, as on 16 September 1920 the aircraft crashed during a test flight. Its pilot, 19-year old pchor. Mieczysław Piniński was killed[8].

On 8 September 1920 the Head of Field Aviation assigned another DH 9 to 6 Eskadra, H4315 overhauled in Warsaw. It arrived at Lwów by rail and upon assembly, on 18 September was assigned to the unit. Three days later the Eskadra returned the aircraft to III RPL after an engine failure.

By that time most of the DH 9s damaged previously had been sent back from Lwów to CSL in Warsaw. On 23 September 1920 III RPL had only three aircraft: D1325, H4315 and the crashed D1275. These remained at Lwów until early next year. D1275 and D1325 were

DH-9, D1273 after landing in the Seret river, July 1920.

(T. Kopański)

DH-9s of 6 Eskadra Wywiadowcza were used against Budionny's cavalry. In the photo is aircraft no D 1275 at Lwów airfield, September 1920.
(T. Kopański)

DH-9 after repair in Centralne Warsztaty Lotnicze in Warsaw, spring 1921. Upper surfaces painted in one - Dark Green colour.
(A. Glass).

sent back to CSL on 28 February 1921, and H4315 in April.

During the early months of 1921 there were at least 17 DH 9s in Poland (mostly dismantled and waiting for repairs). These machines were gradually overhauled at CWL in Warsaw, where they would receive Polish serials beginning with type designation “26”.

In early 1920s these were allocated to 5 Eskadra Wywiadowcza of 3 Pułk Lotniczy in Poznań and to OSOL observers school at Toruń. The latter establishment received four more DH 9s in 1921, these not being made airworthy until August 1923. Five more aircraft withdrawn from 3 Pułk Lotniczy reached OSOL by the end of the year. These aircraft were later used by the training eskadra of 4 Pułk Lotniczy, formed at Toruń upon disbandment of the OSOL school in May 1924. 4 Pułk Lotniczy had, among others, a DH 9 fitted with a

Two shots of the DH-9s of Oficerska Szkoła Obserwatorów Lotniczych in Toruń. Aircraft with "new" Polish markings and Polish number 26.17 (26 indicated DH-9 and next two digits are individual aircraft number). Early 1920s.
(W. Bączkowski) - upper shot
(T. Kopański) - lower shot

In 1923 9 DH-9 were overhauled in Centralne Zakłady Lotnicze . Five of them were sold to Estonia. The aircraft in the photo are without national markings.
(T. Kopański)

Airco DH 9

Two shots of the DH-9 no 26.14 of 4 PL. Aircraft was damaged at Toruń in 1924.
(T. Kopański)

230 hp (169 kW) Austro-Daimler engine. This new power plant was fitted in 1924 at the WCZL workshops in Warsaw.

On 23 December 1923 the Polish Air Force still had seventeen DH 9s, including 10 serviceable ones. The rest had no engines, or were earmarked for cannibalisation (3 aircraft). Five from among these were sold to Estonia in 1924. The new owners allocated them serials in the range from 67 to 71.

Polish DH 9s continued to fly in 4 Pułk Lotniczy until July 1925. Subsequently they were stored, and then written-off. The last aircraft was struck off charge at Toruń in February 1929.

DH.9 A no. F1010 was acquired by Poland after World War II. The aircraft, formerly of no. 110 Squadron RAF, had been forced to land in Germany on 5 October 1918. It was then displayed at the Berlin Aviation Museum. Evacuated to Polish territory during WWII, it was stored near Poznań. From 1963 it was at the Muzeum Lotnictwa Polskiego in Cracow. On 15 June 1977 it was exchanged with the RAF Museum (Hendon) for a Spitfire XVI.

This DH-9A was in custody. The aircraft was stored in Air Museum in Berlin and during WWII all the exhibits were moved to Eastern part of Germany— now Polish territory. After war the DH-9 was captured by Polish soldiers. In 1977 the DH-9 was exchanged with the RAF Museum in Hendon for the Spitfire LF XVI. In the photo fuselage of the last Polish DH-9A just before leaving Muzeum Lotnictwa Polskiego in Cracow.
(MLP)

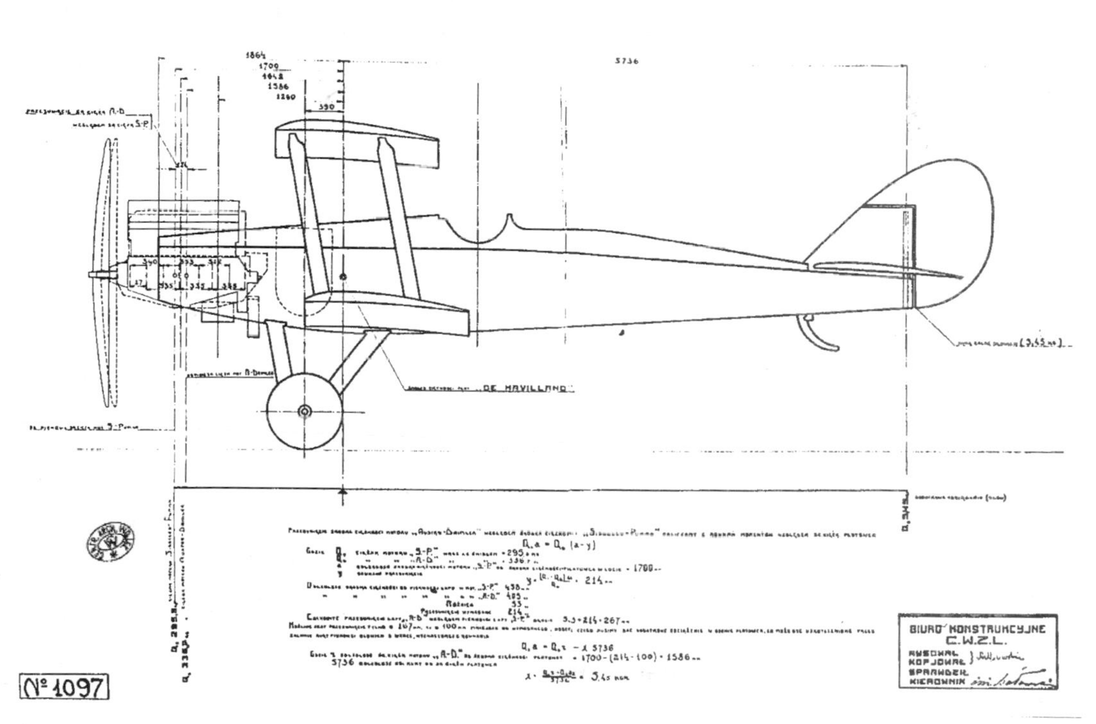

Engine replacement planned by Polish engineers. Change from Siddeley Puma to Austro Daimler engine. Original drawing from CAW archive.

Table no 6. Shipment of DH9 to Poland

Ship Date of departure from London	Shipment	Arrival at Gdańsk	Arrival at Warsaw	Arrival at Lwów
s/s "Neptun" 1/4/1920	2 DH 9s F1173 H4279	approx. 10-15/4/1920	approx. 19/4/1920	19/5/1920
s/s "Warszawa" 21/4/1920	8 DH 9s D1081 D1258 D3242 E9002 E9031 F1174 H4259 H4262	4/5/1920	approx. 10/5/1920	—
s/s "Neptun" 3/5/1920	10 DH 9s* D1237 D1275 D1278 D1325 D5733 F1217 H4260 H4315 H5702 H5721 5 Siddeley Puma engines	11/5/1920	—	27/5/1920

* These aircraft were originally earmarked for the Volunteer Army of Gen. Anton Denikin

R. A. F. RE 8

Only one RAF RE 8 reached Poland as a war prize. It was aircraft no. F3680, manufactured by Daimler Co. Ltd at Coventry (engine no. 4843). The aircraft used to belong to the RAF South Russian Instructional Mission, and after the British left Russia it was taken over by the Bolsheviks at Taganrog. It was allocated to the 36th Reconnaissance Aviaotryad of Budenny's Horse Army air group.

RE-8, serial no F3680, of the 36 Aviaotryad. It made an emergency landing and was captured by Polish troops in Kiev, 5th June 1920. Pilot Sergeyev was captured, but later escaped. Fate of the observer is unknown.
(T. Kopański)

On 5 June 1920 the aircraft made an emergency landing in Kiev which was in Polish hands by that time. It was slightly damaged during landing. .

Personnel of the Kiev-based Polish 3 Eskadra Wywiadowcza disassembled the aircraft and sent it back to Warsaw. The RE 8 arrived at CWL on 14 June 1920, but it was decided there that it would not be feasible to repair it, and it was earmarked to be written-off.

The RE-8 on the truck. The Staff of 3 Eskadra Wywiadowcza loaded the aircraft. Kiev, June 1920.
(T. Kopański)

RAF RE-8 serial no F3680 of 36 Aviaotryad captured by the Poles.
All upper surfaces Dark Green, Undersurfaces - natural fabric.
Rudder - red.
Soviet national markings red star in the white circle.

Avro 504K

The Polish Air Force had a single Avro 504K (British serial unknown). The source of the machine is not clear. Russian documents fail to mention loss of such aircraft during the war against Poland[9]. It seems most probable that the aircraft was purchased from Britain.

The first mention of the aircraft in documents was made on 28 May 1923, when it was test flown at Warsaw-Mokotów airfield. On 19 June of that year it was assigned to the Experimental Section of the Military Air Research Centre in Warsaw. During winter 1923/1924 the aircraft was slightly damaged during a landing. Soon after that it was donated by the military to the Warsaw Technical University as an educational aid for airframe construction studies. It was later used for the same purpose by the Air and Gas Defence League.

The only Avro 504K used in the Polish Air Force. The aircraft was damaged during landing at Mokotów airfield in Warsaw.

(T. Kopański)

HP 0/400

In the second half of 1919 the Poles decided to start civil air communication. National Society for Aerial Navigation in Poland was established to that end. On 16 September 1919 its representatives, together with the British company of Handley Page, presented the Polish Government with an offer to deliver six Handley Page 0/400 aircraft converted to airliners.

The offer was accepted and on 10 December 1919 the first Handley Page with civil registration G-EAMD (ex-D4633) took off from Cricklewood for Poland. The journey in 5 stages (via Brussels, Cologne, Berlin and Poznań) took until 20 December. The aircraft was flown by F/Lt E. D. C. Herne and F/Lt F. G. MacNaught-Davis. They were accompanied by a Polish officer and three British fitters.

In January 1920 the aircraft was presented to the Polish aviation authorities. Mjr pil. Sergiusz Abżółtowski, the acting Head of Field Aviation, took part in one of the

HP 0/400 in Zeppelin hangar, Poznań, December 1919, (T. Kopański)

acquaintance flights. He considered the aircraft easy to fly and supposed that it could be useful not only as an airliner, but also as a warplane.

Aviation HQ was considering establishment of the first Polish destroyer (bomber) eskadra at that time, the unit receiving two Friedrichshafen G.II and one Gotha G.IV aircraft then located in Poznań. Abżółtowski thought that the Handley Page 0/400 could also be allocated to the eskadra (it even had its under-fuselage bomb racks fitted).

In December 1919, HP-0/400, serial HP 28/269, arrived in Poland as a presentation aircraft. This Photo was taken in Poznań, too.
(T. Kopański)

Unfortunately, the Poles failed to reach agreement with the British side on financial questions, and thought that Handley Page asked too much for their aircraft. Eventually the purchase of the aircraft, and importing the remaining five machines, was abandoned.

Some sources say that at the end of 1920 or in early 1921 Handley Page donated the aircraft to the Polish Government. It remained in Warsaw, though, complete-

Another photo of the HP-0/400 in Poznań, December 1919.

(T. Kopański)

ly unused. Every now and then it participated in displays and performed short flights. In January 1922 it underwent an overhaul. It was struck off charge in the early 1920s, and as far as is known it never received Polish markings or civil registration.

HP-0/400 after arrival in Warsaw on 20 December 1919.
(Polish Institute & Sikorski Museum PI&SM)

Different shot taken on the same occasion
(PI&SM)

The HP-0/400 as seen in early spring 1920 at Mokotów airfield. The HP was planned as an airliner in Polish airlines, but that idea was abandoned.
(T. Kopański)

The HP-0/400 at Warsaw 1920
(T. Kopański)

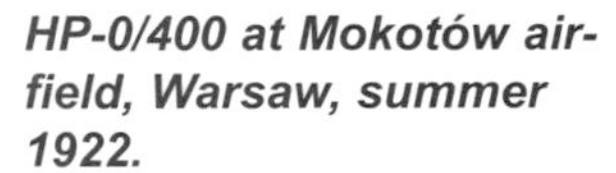

HP-0/400 at Mokotów airfield, Warsaw, summer 1922.
(T. Kopański)

Sopwith 1 1/2 Strutter

The Polish Air Force had three Sopwith 1 1/2 Strutters, all captured during the Polish-Bolshevik war.

The first to be obtained by the Polish was thc British-manufactured Sopwith with serial no. A8744, powered by 120 hp Le Rhone engine no. 9233. The circumstances of its acquisition were rather interesting. On 7th July 1919 the commander of the Bolshevik 3rd Artillery Co-operation Aviaotryad, Juliusz Gilewicz, (Polish born), defected from his unit to the Polish airfield at Nowo Święciany in a Nieuport 24bis fighter. He was accompanied by a Sopwith 1 1/2 Strutter of the same unit. Its crew consisted of: the pilot, S-Lt. Georges Richonier

Sopwith 1 1/2 Strutter no 2326 captured by Polish soldiers at Kowel, September 1920. (W. Bączkowski)

Romanian Sopwith 1 1/2 Strutter at Lewandówka airfield, Lwów, May 1919. (T. Kopański)

(Frenchman) and observer Lt. Pavel Batov (Russian). A large part of the unit's ground crew also defected to the Polish side, as it consisted of many Poles, and anti-Bolshevik Russians.

During landing at Nowo Święciany the Sopwith was slightly damaged. It was repaired by fitters of 1 Eskadra Lotnicza based at Wilno[10], to which the aircraft was allocated. Upon completion of the repair the Sopwith was flown (performing one 10-minute flight). Later on the aircraft was not used in combat, since 1 Eskadra was in the reserve of the Head of Field Aviation.

On 25 August, on the orders of płk. Adam Zaleski, the Head of Field Aviation, the Sopwith 1 1/2 Strutter was despatched to CWL in Warsaw. After inspection płk Zaleski used it as his personal aircraft for visiting his subordinate air units.

In late January 1920 the aircraft suffered an engine failure and, between 20 January and 1 February, it was aggain transferred to CWL. At the turn of February and March 1920, the Sopwith 1 1/2 Strutter was damaged when a hangar collapsed at the Warsaw-Mokotów airfield. According to the directive of the Head of Field Aviation CWL was instructed to repair the aircraft and allocate it to a front-line unit.

Armed with a Lewis observer's machine gun, the 1 1/2 Strutter was test flown on 26 May 1920, and on 1 June it was officially accepted by the receiving commission of the CWL, declaring that the aircraft was in good shape and fit for liaison duties.

On 15 June 1920 the aircraft was assigned to the Aviation HQ of the 1 Army. In early July it left Warsaw for Mołodeczno, where it was allocated to 18 Eskadra Wywiadowcza. For unknown reasons the aircraft was listed in the unit's inventory as Sopwith 4C.6078NA. It still retained its original engine, Le Rhone no. 9233.

On 8 July sierż. pil. Stanisław Śledziejewski with a fitter first flew the aircraft, and the following day they flew it to Lida, to the eskadra airfield. On 13 July 1920 sierż. Śledziejewski with ppor. obs. Marian Sioda departed in the Sopwith for a reconnaissance sortie. After the successful mission an aileron cable broke on the way back, forcing them to land between their own and the Bolshevik lines, and the aircraft was wrecked. As it was not possible to evacuate the seriously damaged Sopwith under enemy fire, only its engine was removed, and the airframe was set on fire.

Another Sopwith 1 1/2 Strutter was captured on 26 June 1920 by 19 Eskadra Myśliwska near Mińsk (in the operational area of the Lithuanian-Byelorussian Front). Its serial number and circumstances of capture are not known. It seems most probable that the aircraft forced-landed near that unit's base. It was perfectly serv-

Romanian Sopwith 1 1/2 Strutter at Lewandówka airfield, Lwów, May 1919. (MLP via Belcarz & Pęczkowski)

Polish and Romanian officers close to Sopwith 1 1/2 Strutter no 916, Lwów, May 1919 (T. Kopański)

iceable and the Poles started to use it immediately for liaison duties.

On 16 July 1920 it took off from Baranowicze airfield to Brześć flown by pchor. pil. Kazimierz Szindler, with ppor pil. Artur Skokowski as a passenger. Soon after take off the aircraft crashed, killing the pilot. Ppor. Skokowski was seriously wounded.

On 12 September 1920 Polish infantry on trucks, escorted by armoured cars, raided Kowel, far behind Bolshevik lines. The action had air support from 8 Eskadra Wywiadowcza in form an aircraft flown by pchor. pil. Aleksander Choinski (most probably an Albatros C.X). The Polish airman arrived over Kowel airfield, and spotting two Bolshevik aircraft at readiness strafed their crews, forcing them to run for cover. Then, with support from the Polish infantry in the town, they landed at the airfield. It turned out that three Bolshevik aircraft were there, including a French-manufactured Sopwith 1 1/2 Strutter no. 2326.

All three machines soon found their way to the II RPL. By 10 October 1920 the Sopwith was sent back to CSL in Warsaw. Its further fate is not known.

Polish airmen flew also other Sopwiths that were not part of the Polish Air Force. Already at the time of the World War I many Polish airmen of the Imperial Russian army had a chance to fly in this type of aircraft. After the

Romanian Sopwith 1 1/2 Strutter. The photo was taken in the last days of May 1919 at Lwów. The aeroplane was briefly used by Polish airmen in May.

(T. Kopański)

war 1 1/2 Strutters also participated in the Russian Civil War. At that time they were also flown by Poles. It is interesting to note that one of them, por. Seweryn Sacewicz, defected from the Bolshevik Air Force to the White Russians in a Sopwith 1 1/2 Strutter.

Sacewicz, like many other officers, was forced to join the Bolsheviks. He was posted to the 36th Reconnaissance Aviaotryad based at Novo-Markovka in the Kantemirov area (southern front). On 31 May 1919, together with an observer, C. M. Vainstein, they took off for a reconnaissance sortie in Sopwith 1 1/2 Strutter no. 6339. Upon crossing the front-line they landed at an airfield of the White Russians. S. Sacewicz later served in the 2 Don Army Aviaotryad until January 1920, subsequently returning to Poland. He was killed in November 1920 in a Bristol Fighter with Polish serial 20.32.

On 27 May 1919 a Romanian liaison Sopwith 1 1/2 Strutter no. 916 landed at the airfield of the III Grupa Lotnicza at Lwów. It stayed at Lwów for three days, and during that time Polish pilots performed several acquaintance flights in it. Kpt. pil. Stefan Bastyr, CO III Grupa Lotnicza, was among the airmen who flew the Rumanian Sopwith.

In early 1920, after the agreement with the Latvian government, the Poles pushed the Bolsheviks from Dyneburg (Daugavpils). During the following weeks Polish and Latvian troops under gen. Edward Rydz-Śmigły continued offensive operations against the Red Army on the northern bank of the Dźwina river. On 21 February 1920 a Bolshevik Sopwith 1 1/2 Strutter no. A5248 from 45th Aviaotryad landed at Rzerzyca (Rezekne), among the Latvian units reporting to gen.

Rydz-Śmigły. The crew consisted of pilot, por. Włodzimierz Korobowski and fitter, Alfons Joniškanis. Gen. Rydz-Śmigły agreed that the aircraft be retained by the Latvians. por. Korobowski joined the Latvian Air Force and later flew the Sopwith in combat against the Bolsheviks.

NOTES

1 **Lwów is now Lviv in Ukraine.**

2 **According to J. M. Bruce the Bristols earmarked for Poland were serialled: E2089, E2093, E2655, E2656, E5282, H1010, H1038, H5952, H5960, H5963**

3 **The aircraft (20.49) was subsequently used by the Bolshevik 2nd, and then 3rd Independent Fighter Flight at Kharkov until at least September 1924.**

4 **Poland thus becoming the second greatest user of these aircraft, after Britain.**

5 **"For all trades" (French.)**

6 **Namely aircraft nos.: 20.5, 20.7, 20.9, 20.10, 20.19, 20.22, 20.23, 20.24, 20.26, 20.28, 20.30, 20.35, 20.37, 20.38, 20.52, 20.59, 20.67, 20.74, 20.75, 20.76, 20.77, 20.79, 20.86, 20.96, 20.99, 20.100, 20.101.**

7 **Kpt. Ciecierski later escaped from custody and in November 1920 returned to Poland.**

8 **Some sources claim that another type of aircraft was involved in this accident.**

9 **Some authors claim incorrectly that the Polish Avro 504K had serial F2326 or H2326. However, both Polish and Russian documents quote the number 2326 as the Sopwith 1 1/2 Strutter captured by the Poles at Kowel in September 1920.**

10 **Wilno is now Vilnius in Lithuania.**

Polish Air Force ranks

Polish Air Force ranks were identical to ranks of the army. Flying personnel were identified by adding the word pilot (pil.) or obserwator (obs. - English observer-navigator).

Polish rank	Polish abbereviation	Direct translation	RAF equivalent
szeregowy	szer.	private	aircraftsman
starszy szeregowy	st. szer.	senior private	leading aircraftsman
kapral	kpr.	corporal	senior aircraftsman
plutonowy	plut.	platoon commander	corporal
sierżant	sierż.	sergeant	sergeant
starszy sierżant	st. sierż.	senior sergeant	flight sergeant
chorąży	chor.	warrant officer	warrant officer
podporucznik	ppor.	sub-lieutenant	pilot officer
porucznik	por.	lieutenant	flying officer
kapitan	kpt.	captain	flight lieutenant
major	mjr	major	squadron leader
podpułkownik	ppłk	sub-colonel	wing commander
pułkownik	płk	colonel	group captain
generał brygady	gen. bryg.	brigadier general	air commodore
generał dywizji	gen. dyw.	divisional general	air vice marshal
generał lotnictwa	gen. lotn.	air force general	air marshal
generał armii	gen. armii	army general	air chief marshal

(courtesy Wojtek Matusiak)

Bibliography

Centralne Archiwum Wojskowe w Warszawie- CAW (Central Military Archive in Warsaw)
- different aviation documents
Material from Russian archives courtesy Marat Chairulin

Chaz Bowyer, Bristol F2B Fighter. King of Two-Seaters, Ian Allan, London 1985.
Jack M. Bruce, The Aeroplanes of the Royal Flying Corps (Military Wing), Putnam, London 1983.
Jack M. Bruce, Avro 504K, Windsock Datafile No 28, Albatros Productions Ltd. 1991.
Jack M. Bruce, Bristol Fighter, Windock Datafile Special, vol 1 and vol 2, Albatros Productions Ltd, 1997, 1998.
Jack M. Bruce, De Havilland Aircraft of World War One, Arms and Armour Press, London 1991.
Jack M. Bruce, DH 9, Windsock Datafile No 71, Albatros Productions Ltd. 1998.
Jack M. Bruce, RAF SE 5a, Windsock Datafile Special, Albatros Productions Ltd. 1993.
Jack M. Bruce, Sopwith Camel, Windsock Datafile No 26, Albatros Productions Ltd. 1991
Jack M. Bruce, Sopwith Dolphin, Windsock Datafile No 54, Albatros Productions Ltd. 1995.
Jack M. Bruce, Sopwith 1 1/2 Strutter, Windsock Datafile No 34, Albatros Productions Ltd. 1992
Tomasz J. Kopański, Brisfits in Poland, Cover story, Windsock International 1995, vol. 11 No 4.
Tomasz J. Kopański, Jak to z SE 5a było ..., Skrzydlata Polska 1994 No 7
Tomasz J. Kopański, Jedyny wielbłąd w Polsce, (dzieje samolotu Camel), Aeroplan 1995 No 2.
Tomasz J. Kopański, Polskie Bristole na wojnie, Militaria 1996, vol. 2, No 2.
Tomasz J. Kopański, Samoloty zdobyczne w wojnie 1919-1920, part 1, Militaria 1992 vol. 2 No 3 and part 2, Militaria 1993, vol. 1 No 4.
Marian Krzyżan, Samoloty w muzeach polskich, Warszawa 1983.
Andrzej Morgała, Samoloty wojskowe w Polsce 1918-1924, Warszawa 1997.
Adam Popiel, Uzbrojenia lotnictwa polskiego 1918-1939, Warszawa 1991.
Bruce Robertson, British Military Aircfraft Serials 1912-1966, Jan Allan, London 1967.

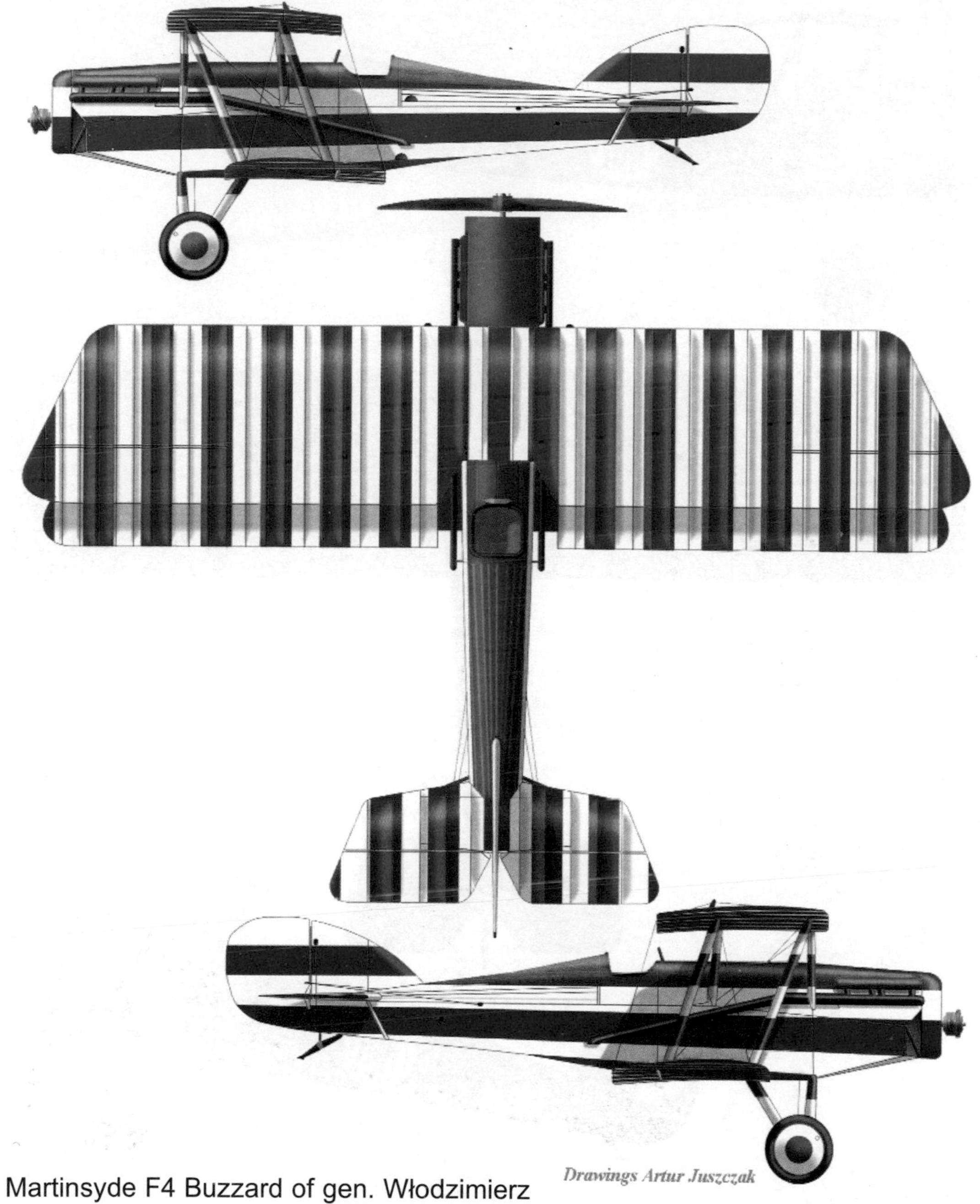

Martinsyde F4 Buzzard of gen. Włodzimierz Zagórski, Warsaw 1926. Aircraft painted in red and white stripes, without national markings or serial.

Sopwith 1 F.1 Camel of 7 Eskadra Myśliwska, Lwów, October 1920.
Aircraft in original British camouflage and British serial with Polish national markings and 7 Eskadra (Kościuszko) badge.

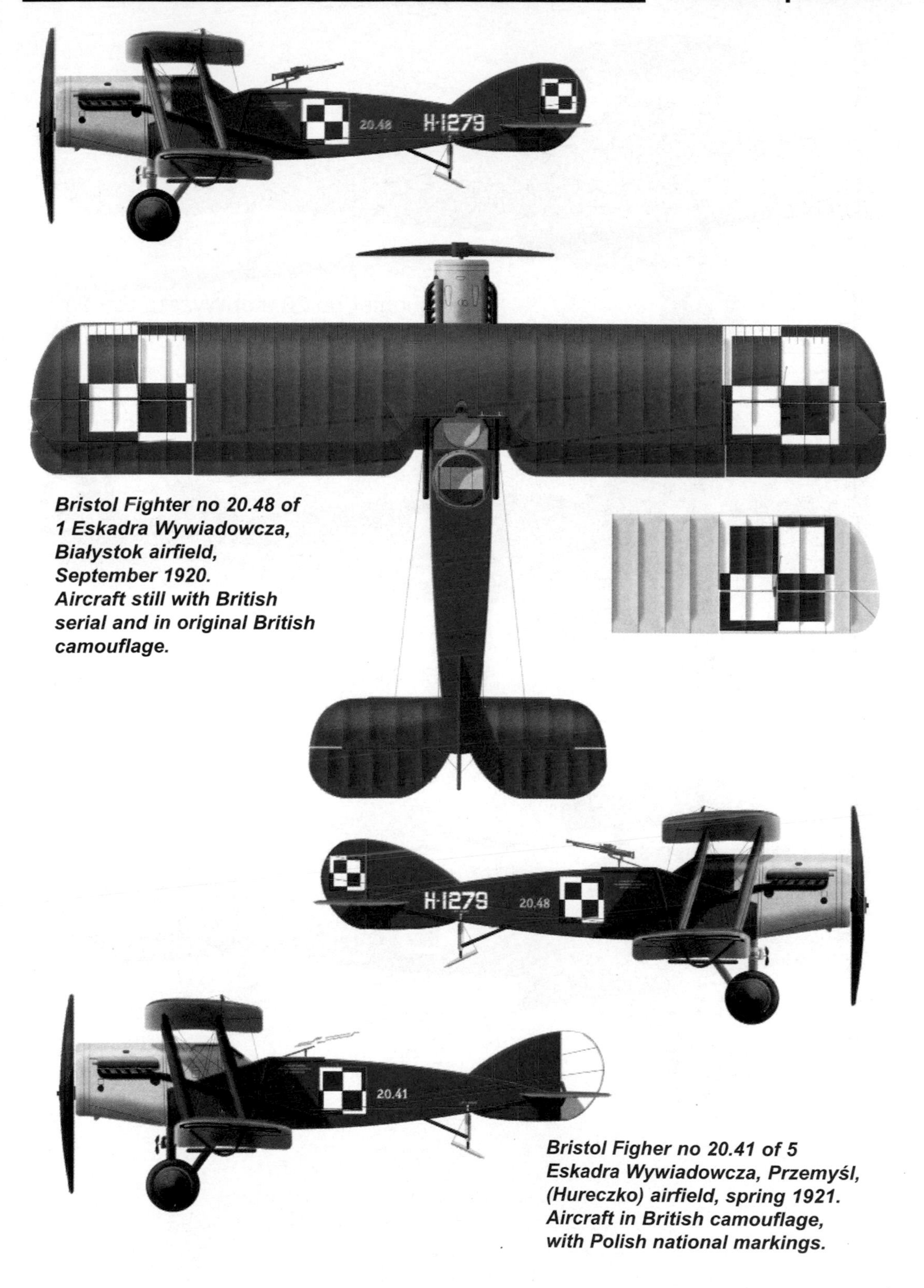

Bristol Fighter no 20.48 of 1 Eskadra Wywiadowcza, Białystok airfield, September 1920. Aircraft still with British serial and in original British camouflage.

Bristol Figher no 20.41 of 5 Eskadra Wywiadowcza, Przemyśl, (Hureczko) airfield, spring 1921. Aircraft in British camouflage, with Polish national markings.

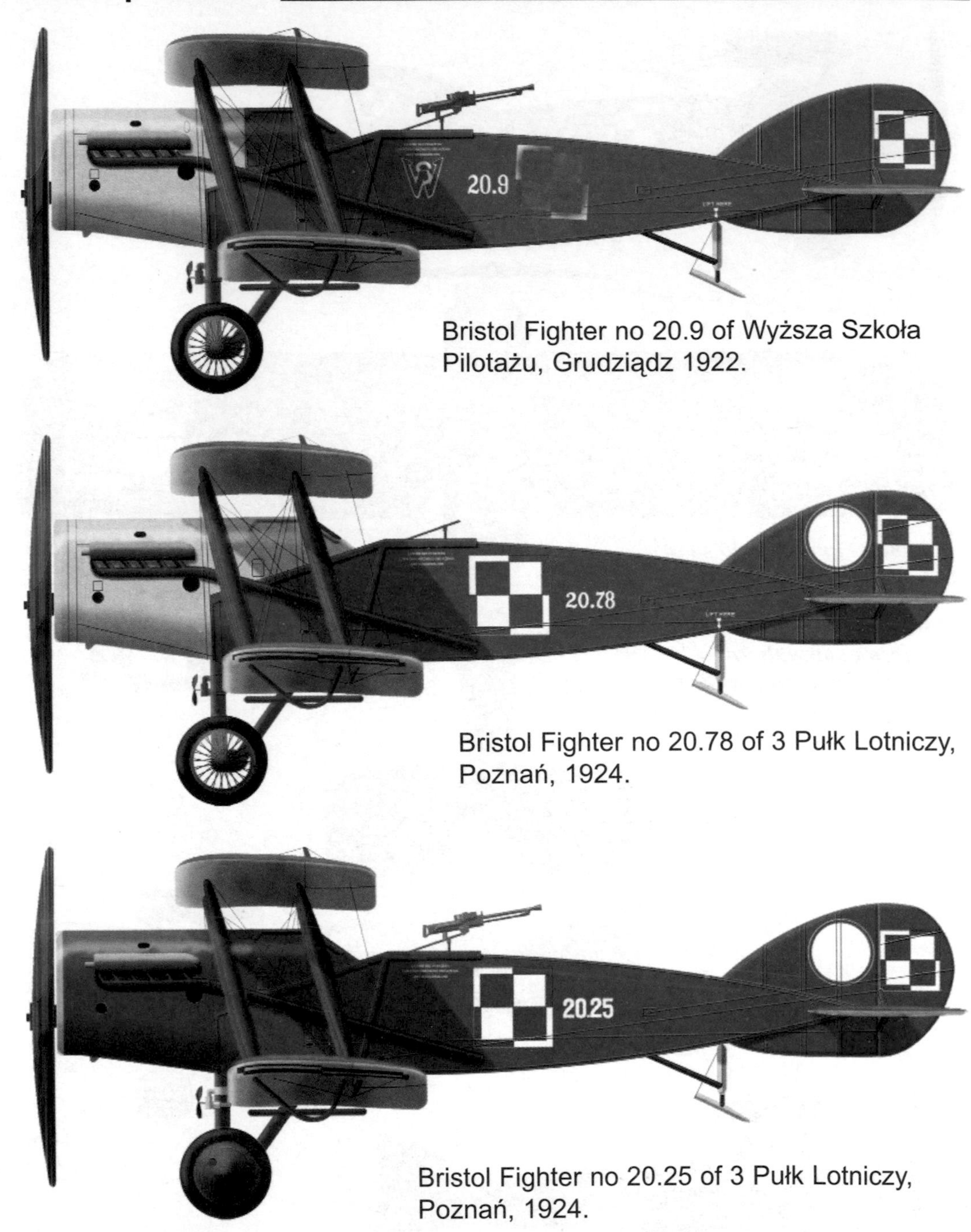

Bristol Fighter no 20.9 of Wyższa Szkoła Pilotażu, Grudziądz 1922.

Bristol Fighter no 20.78 of 3 Pułk Lotniczy, Poznań, 1924.

Bristol Fighter no 20.25 of 3 Pułk Lotniczy, Poznań, 1924.

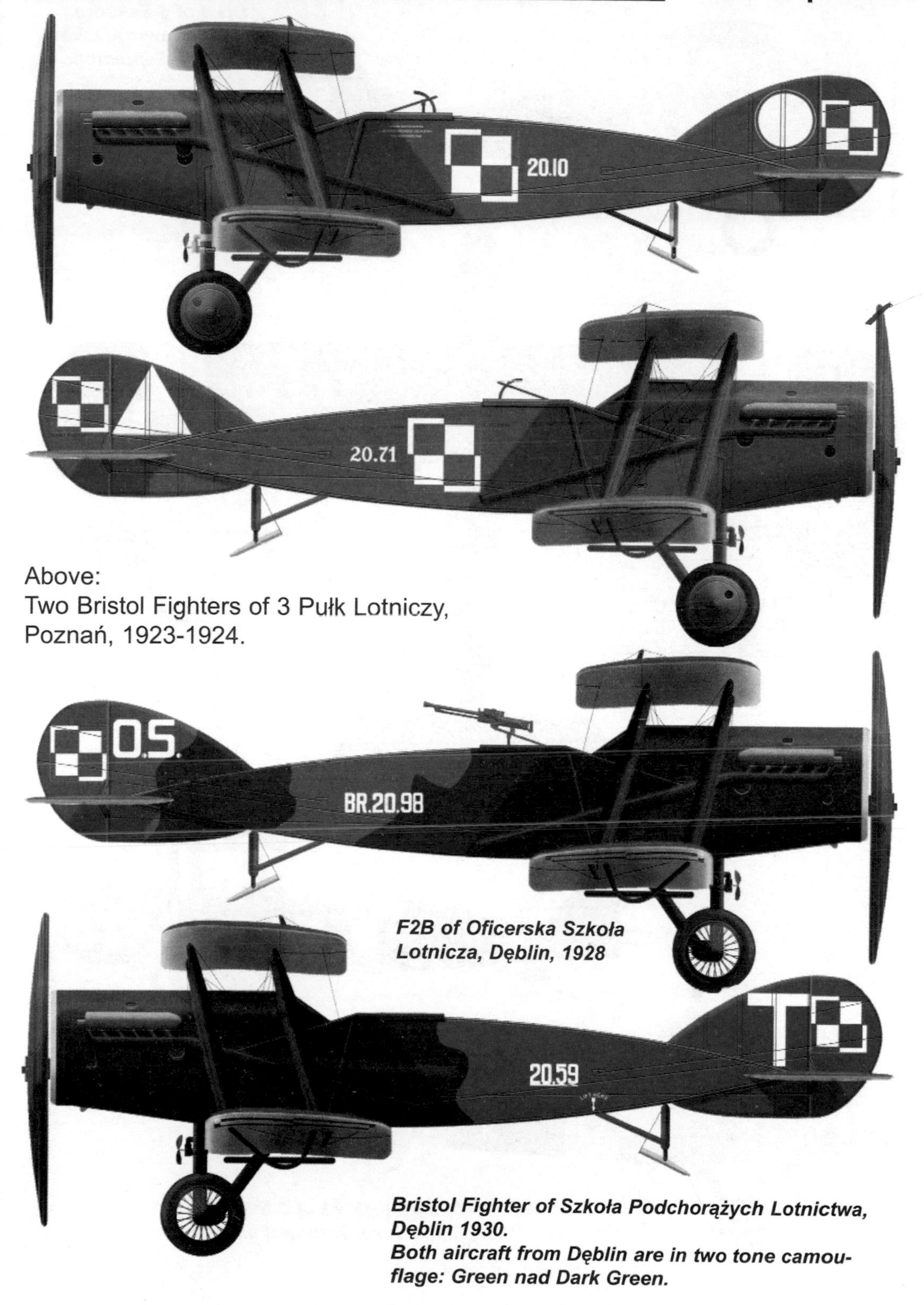

Above:
Two Bristol Fighters of 3 Pułk Lotniczy, Poznań, 1923-1924.

F2B of Oficerska Szkoła Lotnicza, Dęblin, 1928

Bristol Fighter of Szkoła Podchorążych Lotnictwa, Dęblin 1930.
Both aircraft from Dęblin are in two tone camouflage: Green nad Dark Green.

Colour profiles

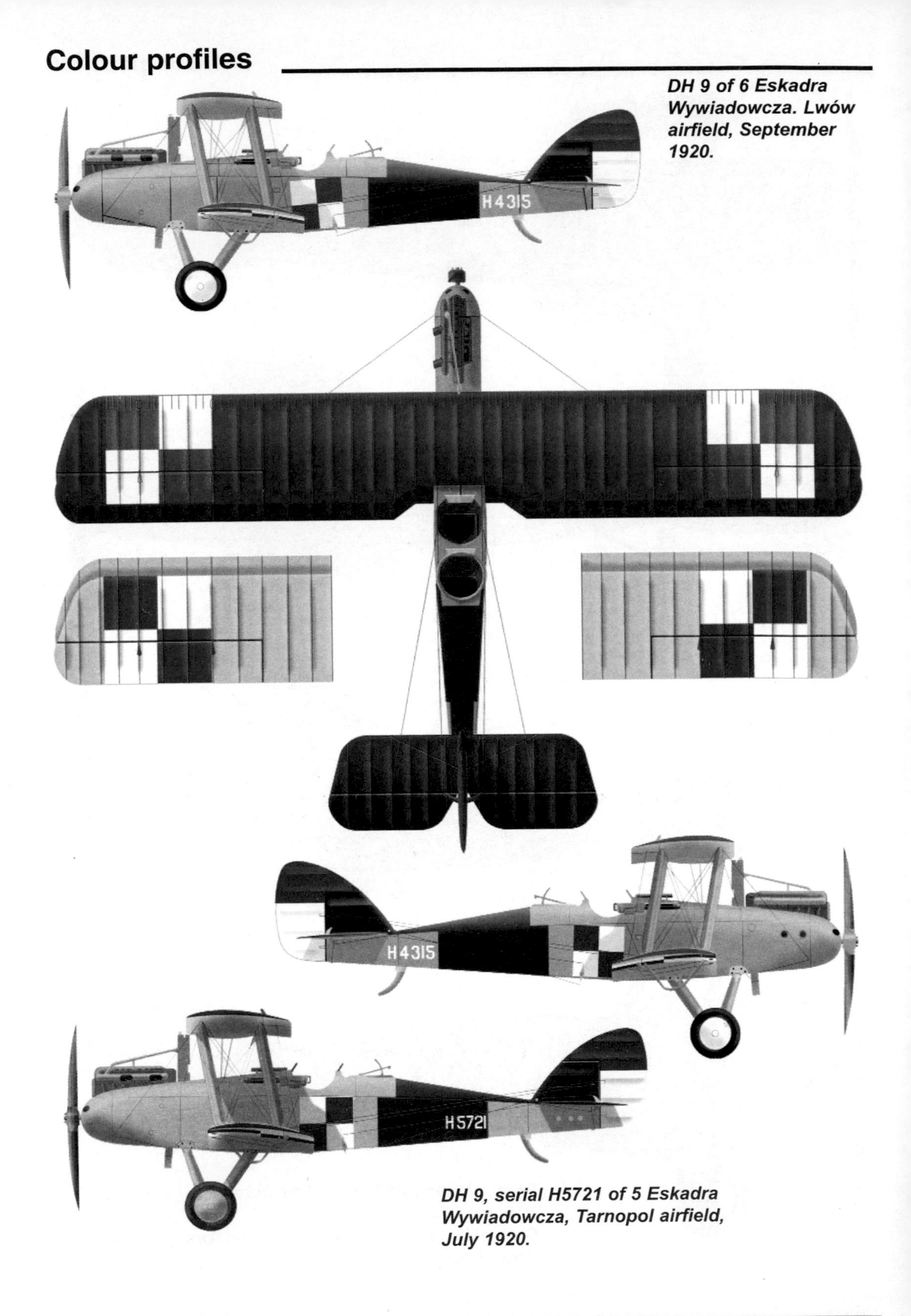

DH 9 of 6 Eskadra Wywiadowcza. Lwów airfield, September 1920.

DH 9, serial H5721 of 5 Eskadra Wywiadowcza, Tarnopol airfield, July 1920.

DH 9 no 26.17 and no 26.14 of 4 Pułk Lotniczy, Toruń airfield, 1924.
Both aircraft repainted after overhaul. Upper surfaces in Dark Green, lower in natural fabric colour.

SE 5a no 12.01 of 7 Eskadra Myśliwska, Hołoby airfield, 15 July 1920. Aircraft in original British camouflage.

SE 5a of Savage Skywriting Co., Poland 1926. Aircraft painted in silver overall

HP 0/400, G-EAMD, Warsaw, Mokotów airfield, December 1919.

20.17